AF472403

Actively WAITING

WHAT TO DO BETWEEN THE PROMISE GIVEN AND THE PROMISE FULFILLED

LYLE GRIMES

Copy Edited by: Rachel Starr Thomson
Contact information: followerforever@hotmail.com - http://rachelstarrthomson.blogspot.com

Layout and pagination designed by Visual Offerings, Inc.
6834 Cantrell Road PMB 407, Little Rock, Arkansas 72207
info@visualofferings.com

All scripture quotations, unless otherwise indicated, are taken from the New King James Version®. Copyright © 1982 by Thomas Nelson, Inc. Used by permission. All rights reserved.

WARNING CONCERNING COPYRIGHT RESTRICTIONS © 2006 Lyle Grimes
The copyright law of the United States (Title 17, United States Code) governs the making of photocopies or other reproduction of copyrighted material. Under certain conditions specified in the law, libraries and archives are authorized to furnish a photocopy or other reproduction. One of these specified conditions is that the photocopy or reproduction is not to be used for any purpose other than private study, scholarship, or research. If electronic transmission of reserve material is used for purposes in excess of what constitutes "fair use," that user may be liable for copyright infringement.

Table of CONTENTS

Introduction HURRY UP AND WAIT

How many times have you heard the saying "hurry up and wait"? How many times have you said it yourself? Most people view waiting as a punishment or an ordeal that has to be endured. The world we live in today reinforces this viewpoint by trying to move at breakneck speed to instant gratification. This trend has caused us to forget how to wait.

Waiting has been around for thousands of years and it will have a part in each of our lives. This being the case, we can deal with waiting in one of two ways: we can dread it, or we can discover what God wants us to learn through it.

Throughout the Bible examples can be found of God's people waiting for promises to be fulfilled. David had to wait to be King, the Children of Israel waited to see the Promised Land, and the Church is still waiting for Christ's return.

Today, it seems that everyone is waiting for something. Some people are waiting for a spouse, for a new job, for loved ones to return, or for financial freedom. The list could go on forever, but the fact is, waiting is woven into the fabric of our lives.

The only question is, how will we wait?

You may have heard that it is best to wait patiently, however, in this book we will look at how we can actively wait on the promises God has given us.. We will look at the hardships, trials, joys, and adventures of the Jewish people as they waited for God to deliver them to the Promised Land. We will also see how the lessons they learned along the way can help us as we go through the waiting periods of our lives.

Are you ready to start Actively Waiting?

Chapter 1
SECURING GOD'S PROMISE

For He remembered His holy promise, And Abraham His servant.
Psalm 105:42

We will begin our journey by asking this important question: what are you waiting for?

Genesis 12 tells the story of one who knew why he was waiting:

The summer breeze blew gently over the plains as a man looked out over the hillside. His mind was filled with thoughts of his father, who had recently departed this life. He still remembered thinking his father would live forever. Yet, death had come and shattered his childhood illusions. As his mind wandered, he found himself asking questions that he'd never had the courage to ask while his father was alive.

He wondered why his father had uprooted his family so many years ago. Why had he brought them to this place? He and his family had lived here now for many years. Though the years had come and gone, this land had never felt like home.

The truth was, he still felt like a stranger in a foreign land. It was this thought that held his mind for some time. A loud voice startled him as it invaded his mind and jolted him back to reality.

"Abraham."

Someone had just called his name, but who?

He turned around to see who had called out to him, but there was no one there. Then the voice called out again, and this time he knew deep within who the voice belonged to.

"Get out of your country, From your family And from your father's house, To a land that I will show you."

(Genesis 12:1)

In the next few moments God gave him a promise that was far beyond his wildest imagination. God spoke to Abraham and said:

"I will make you a great nation; I will bless you And make your name great; And you shall be a blessing. I will bless those who bless you, And I will curse him who curses you; And in you all the families of the earth shall be blessed"

(Genesis 12:2-3)

As he stood there, the reality of this promise poured over him. Visions of the future soon filled his mind and, from that moment on, he never allowed himself to doubt. Instead he chose to believe fully in the words of God.

In that moment Abraham was given a promise from God that would affect not only his life but also the lives of people he would never know. In response to this promise, Abraham left his home and followed God. God promised and Abraham obeyed: simple, yet profound.

HAVE YOU EVER RECEIVED A PROMISE ABOUT YOUR FUTURE?

Throughout my life I have given and received many promises. The first promise I can remember was given to me by my father. As a child I would play football every Saturday. Each week I would ask my father if he was coming to my game and he would answer, "Yes." I always responded with yet another question: "Do you promise?" His response was always, "Yes, I'll be there."

Growing up, I learned early on that there was nothing greater than a promise from a father to his son. When my father said he would do something, his word was his bond. If he committed to something, he stayed committed--no matter what the cost.

This lesson was reinforced each time I looked out from the football field and saw my father standing on the sidelines. He said he would be there, and he was. My faith in my father's promises rose each time he stood there and cheered me on.

The one promise I remember above all others came from God. It was a time in my life when I was trying to find my own way. I found myself struggling with God's call on my life. Deep inside I knew that I was not living for the purpose for which I was created.

I felt a strong call to be active in the ministry; however, I wanted to find my future in politics. At an early age, I fell in love with President Ronald Reagan, and all I wanted to do was follow in his footsteps. Even as a young boy I could see myself as a future Senator from Texas.

That was all fine and good until I attended a church camp when I was twelve years old. I can remember the event as if it had happened this past week. I felt the Lord move on me like never before. During the week I felt compelled to spend quiet times on my knees in prayer. It was during one of these times that I knew I had heard the call God had placed on my life.

For the next several years, my soul fought with my flesh. It's funny now, but I can remember trying to make deals with God. I would tell him I would be happy to serve as the Chaplain for the Senate, but I still desired to be a US Senator. He never condemned me; He just continued to move my heart closer to His will.

One night as I dreamed, I saw the future God has for me. I was overwhelmed, because it was more than I could ever have wished for. When I awoke I prayed earnestly, and I felt God telling me that if I was willing to let Him, He would fulfill His plans for my life.

At that moment, God gave me a promise and I responded. Since that time, I have experienced many things along the road He has chosen for me. Some of them I would not wish to repeat, but even in those times I know God was there. Each time I thought that I could not go on, God delivered me. The rewards were always worth the trials.

One of the most valuable lessons I have learned along the way is that God is perfect, and I am not. This means when He makes a promise, He will keep it. I have failed many times to keep promises, but He has never failed to keep one. You can rest assured that if He has given you a promise, He will fulfill it.

Now, let me ask you once more: do you have a promise from God? If not, then that is the first thing you need to seek. God has a promise for each of us, a promise greater than any of us can imagine. Your very life is a promise and only He can share with you what your future holds. Seek Him and He will answer. Then it's up to you to respond to Him.

As you respond, you will begin a journey that will take you to your promise. For some, the journey may be short, while for others it may take many years. During your walk with God, you will find that as you reach one promise God already has another waiting for you. You will have some promises that will cover short spans of time while others will take a lifetime to fulfill.

No matter what your journey looks like, it will include a great deal of waiting. Yet, no matter how long it takes to reach the end, you will know why you are waiting.

YOU CAN REST ASSURED THAT IF HE HAS GIVEN YOU A PROMISE, HE WILL FULFILL IT.

In this book I hope to show you many things that you may encounter along the way, to help you prepare for the journey. However, please keep in mind that the timing of your journey will depend on a few things:

1. **The larger the dream, the more time it will take to prepare you for it.**
2. **Your willingness to conform to God's ways and lay your ways aside.**
3. **Your willingness to fully trust in God's plan for your life.**
4. **Your willingness to obey God fully.**
5. **God's ultimate timing.**

This list has not covered every aspect of this journey, nor will this book cover everything you will experience as you go from the promise to its fulfillment. Instead, I hope this book will serve as a guide to help you along the way.

I know from personal experience that waiting for the fulfillment of a promise can be a long process. However, it helps to know that God is there with you every step of the way. If He has given you a promise, He will cause it to come to pass.

SECURING GOD'S PROMISE

Genesis 12:1-5

1 Now the LORD had said to Abram: "Get out of your country, From your family And from your father's house, To a land that I will show you. 2 I will make you a great nation; I will bless you And make your name great; And you shall be a blessing. 3 I will bless those who bless you, And I will curse him who curses you; And in you all the families of the earth shall be blessed." 4 So Abram departed as the LORD had spoken to him, and Lot went with him. And Abram was seventy-five years old when he departed from Haran. 5 Then Abram took Sarai his wife and Lot his brother's son, and all their possessions that they had gathered, and the people whom they had acquired in Haran, and they departed to go to the land of Canaan. So they came to the land of Canaan.

Hebrews 6:13-15

13 For when God made a promise to Abraham, because He could swear by no one greater, He swore by Himself, 14 saying, "Surely blessing I will bless you, and multiplying I will multiply you." 15 And so, after he had patiently endured, he obtained the promise.

Review Questions:

1. What dreams do you have for your future?

____

____

____

____

____

2. Are these dreams yours or God's?

____

____

____

____

____

3. What are the promises that God has given you?

4. Are you willing to lay your dreams down for God's?

5. What are you willing to give to receive God's promises for your life?

Chapter 2

50 MILES FROM NOWHERE AND STILL GOING STRONG

He found him in a desert land And in the wasteland, a howling wilderness; He encircled him, He instructed him, He kept him as the apple of His eye.
Deuteronomy 32:10

The sun rose on another routine day for the old weary shepherd. Every day was the same in his life. He awoke with the sun, took care of the sheep, and returned to his home at night. He had walked every trail, passed every tree, and climbed every hill in this wilderness a thousand times over.

He began this day as the many days before, reflecting on his life. Many years had passed since he had first lead his sheep to this hillside. The life he'd left behind was now in the distant past. He stood looking at himself in the reflection of the watering hole. The man he used to be was far different from the man that now stared back at him. He knew that many more years lay ahead, and he wondered what kind of man he would become. Would he always work for others, or did God have a plan for his life?

He had no idea how different this day would be from those that had come before. The day would soon prove to be one of the most pivotal of his life. For today, he would have an encounter with God that would transform his very being.

As he stood thinking, he noticed a flicker of light in the distance. The light seemed strange and out of place. As he drew closer to the light he noticed that it came from a fire. "How strange," he thought. No one but his tribe lived in this area. Who would have started a fire?

His curiosity soon got the best of him and he set out to find what was burning. As he approached the fire, his curiosity at first was quenched. It was simply a bush that was burning and nothing more. Just then the reality before him set in. The bush was on fire, yet it was not being consumed.

His mind was at war with itself. He tried with logic to grasp at an answer, yet, none could be found. Fire consumes wood. There is no way around it. How then was this bush burning but not being consumed? Before his mind could direct his next thought, he heard a voice coming from the bush. Frozen by the voice, he was warned not to come any closer. The voice told him that where he now stood was holy ground. At that moment, deep within his spirit, he realized he was hearing the voice of God.

There, in the middle of the vast wilderness, Moses had an encounter with God. There was nothing to distract him or to compete with his senses. He was alone with God, and all of his attention was given to the moment.

GOD DOES NOT WANT TO COMPETE WITH THE OTHER THINGS IN OUR LIVES; HE WANTS TO BE THE CENTER OF OUR ATTENTION.

Why did God not meet with Moses in the village, or while others were around? For that matter, why does He not often meet with us in such settings? One reason may be that, though God wants to meet us in our daily lives, He has to compete with the distractions of our lives. God could meet us anywhere, but He has also given us free will. Therefore, we have to choose where to focus our time and attention. God does not want to compete with the other things in our lives; He wants to be the center of our attention.

It is also important to point out that it was in the wilderness that God laid out the true purpose of Moses' life. The encounter with God shifted Moses' entire being and set him on a course that would lead to the freedom of millions. God called out to Moses and he responded with a humble heart.

Have you ever gotten away from everything in life? When was the last time you spent quiet time before the Lord with no distractions? If you want to know the plan God has for your life, or if you want direction along the way, it is vital for you to spend time listening to the voice of God. He created you, and He alone knows your true purpose. He knows your desires and He knows His plan for your life.

God wants to meet with you where you are, be it in the city or out in the wilderness. God met me on the back roads of Texas and the encounter changed my life forever.

A thousand miles of highway lay between Austin and Albuquerque, New Mexico, stretching through the vast open lands of West Texas. Most people would be satisfied with taking the interstate, or at least the state highways, but this trip I wanted to do something a little different.

The route I chose would bypass most of the small towns that populate the state highways of Texas. My thought in planning which road to take was simple: I would choose the one with the least amount of towns. This way, instead of small town traffic lights and speed traps, I would have open roads and nothing to slow me down. There was one small fact that did slip my mind: fewer small towns also meant fewer places to purchase gas. This probably would have occurred to most people after the first sign that read "Next stop for gas 100 miles ahead." I wish I could say I was smart enough to catch on. However, when I read those words the only thought in my mind was that there was nothing but an open road for the next hundred miles.

For the first twenty miles I listened to the local radio station. My foot eased down on the accelerator, and I got comfortable in my seat. As the wind blew through the car, I could think of nothing but how wonderful life seemed to be. As the miles passed, the signal on the radio began to fail. I knew it was only a matter of time until the music that now filled the air would fall silent.

As the music finally gave way to silence, I realized I was still sixty miles from the next town. There I sat with only the sound of the wind flowing through the car. My mind turned from enjoying the moment to wondering about the larger things of life. Where was I in my life? What was my destination? What things would I do or see along the way?

The most probing question was this: who was I living my life for? The question seemed to be spoken out of the air, as if it had traveled in on the very wind that now rushed around me. Who was I living my life for? I wanted to say for God, of course, yet my soul would not let me. Was I truly living for God, or was I only living for myself and playing the good Christian when it seemed appropriate? Was I a fraud, a fake? When I began to honestly examine my life, I realized there were still many areas of my life that I had yet to surrender to God.

I was on the way to rebuilding my life on Christ. Yet, I had not reached the point where I truly trusted God with every part of my life. As I examined my heart and my deepest thoughts, I felt God's compassion and grace flow over me. There was not a moment that I felt condemned or pressured by God. Gently, I felt His hand move through my heart, dividing my ways and my desires from His.

As He did so, I knew I was being changed. He was slowly transforming me into His image. I knew that just as Albuquerque, NM still lay in the distance, so did my final destination with God. Finally, I knew that while my car was fifty miles from the next stop, I was heading in the right direction. And at last I knew that the same was true for my spiritual life. I was fifty miles from nowhere, but I was still going strong.

Going into the desert and searching for a burning bush is not the only way to hear God. Nor do you have to escape to the wilderness or leave your life to find Him—or to "find yourself," or to discover meaning in your life. However, you should always be open to the voice of God.

GOD WANTS TO MEET WITH YOU WHERE YOU ARE, BE IT IN THE CITY OR OUT IN THE WILDERNESS.

Most of us live very active lives, and it can be difficult to find a place of listening. There are some practical things that can be done to help quiet your environment. You can start by turning your radio off while driving, or spending five minutes in the morning in silence. These things will not be easy at first. The quiet times may be difficult. We are so used to having multiple distractions that we have to train ourselves to be silent and listen to God. I suggest starting off small with just a few minutes and then building from there. God knows that change happens over time, but a journey cannot be completed if the first step is never taken.

50 MILES FROM NOWHERE AND STILL GOING STRONG

1 Samuel 3:1-3

*1 Then the boy Samuel ministered to the LORD before Eli. And the word of the LORD was rare in those days; there was no widespread revelation. 2
And it came to pass at that time, while Eli was lying down in his place, and when his eyes had begun to grow so dim that he could not see, 3 This man went up from his city yearly to worship and sacrifice to the LORD of hosts in Shiloh. Also the two sons of Eli, Hophni and Phinehas, the priests of the LORD, were there.*

1 Samuel 3:10

10 Now the LORD came and stood and called as at other times, "Samuel! Samuel!" And Samuel answered, "Speak, for Your servant hears."

Exodus 3:1-6

*1 Now Moses was tending the flock of Jethro his father-in-law, the priest of Midian. And he led the flock to the back of the desert, and came to Horeb, the mountain of God. 2 And the Angel of the LORD appeared to him in a flame of fire from the midst of a bush. So he looked, and behold, the bush was burning with fire, but the bush was not consumed. 3 Then Moses said, "I will now turn aside and see this great sight, why the bush does not burn."
4 So when the LORD saw that he turned aside to look, God called to him from the midst of the bush and said, "Moses, Moses!" And he said, "Here I am." 5 Then He said, "Do not draw near this place. Take your sandals off your feet, for the place where you stand is holy ground." 6 Moreover He said, "I am the God of your father -- the God of Abraham, the God of Isaac, and the God of Jacob." And Moses hid his face, for he was afraid to look upon God.*

Review Questions:

1. Am I ready to meet God?

____

____

____

____

____

2. What will my response be when He calls my name?

3. Am I willing to let God to change my heart?

4. How can I begin today to nourish an environment that is welcoming to God?

5. Am I heading in the right direction?

6. Do I have short-term goals and destinations that are moving me closer to Your promise?

Chapter 3
ACCEPTING AMAZEMENT

A present is a precious stone in the eyes of its possessor;
Wherever he turns, he prospers.
Proverbs 17:8

The man from the desert had arrived sometime ago. Egypt, did not heed his warnings or his request, though they knew him well. They ridiculed him--until the words he spoke came to pass.

One tragedy after another struck the mightiest nation in the world. They had trained to defend against any earthly army, but no training could teach them to fight against the unseen hand that now struck against them. They sacrificed and prayed, but their gods seemed helpless in protecting them against the ongoing attacks.

All of the fields that had once been ripe now stood desolate. Herds of livestock were destroyed and terrible diseases engulfed the population. The nation's leader assured his people that these trials would pass, and that everything would return to normal. While they wanted to believe him, they could not escape the reality before them. The ending of one wave of destruction only seemed to be the beginning of another. How much worse could it become? How long could this mighty nation stand before it crumbled under the destruction that assailed it?

The answer came in a single night. It was hailed by the cries of millions as, throughout the land, men of all ages fell to the cold hand of death. As the sun rose the next day, it was apparent that only the slaves had not suffered loss—only the Hebrew slaves, whose cause the man from the desert championed.

With each plague, the results were the same. The citizens suffered and the slaves were not harmed. The desert man, Moses, continued to tell Egypt's leader that if only he would free the slaves, the suffering would end. This, however, was something the leader had decided could never be done. How would his empire continue to prosper without slave labor? How would the mighty buildings be built or the crops harvested?

The leader remained steadfast against letting the slaves go. However, on the night that death passed through the land, the leader's guards, spiritual advisers, even his gods could not protect him. He held his firstborn son in his arms as the boy died. With the passing of his son, the leader decided that his heart could take no more.

He ordered the slaves out of his sight forever. Moses told the slaves to prepare to leave the country immediately. He also told them to ask the citizens of the nation for gold and silver as they departed. The slaves followed his instructions to the letter, and in an instant went from slavery to freedom.

The departing slaves found favor in the eyes of the Egyptians, who gave them gold, silver, jewelry, and other items, making the slaves not only free, but abundantly blessed.

The children of Israel had two options at this moment. As these events unfolded, the slaves had to either accept God's blessings or reject them. Some accepted them fully, but others tried to hang on to their old life even as they stepped into the new. When trouble came to them in the desert, they begged to be allowed to go back to Egypt. In spirit, some rejected the blessings of God.

Why would they do such a thing? They had only known slavery and poverty for generations—perhaps they thought it was too good to be true. In one day, they not only received their freedom, but also prosperity. Many times when God blesses us, it comes in an instant and it is up to us to accept it or to reject it.

Has God ever presented you with an opportunity that looked too good to be true? Did you turn it down or accept it? Did you not enjoy it because you were always worried about what could happen to take it away? Many times, when we receive something amazing from God we have a tendency to treat it skeptically, or else we try desperately to keep it in our own power. We become so worried that it may disappear or be stolen from us that we never experience the fullness of God through it.

One late spring day, I received a call from a couple I had known for several years. They are amazing, and I have watched them live their lives fully serving God. They are real people doing incredible things for God. Through their willingness to be used by God, millions of lives have been touched.

When I heard their voices on the other end of the phone, a smile stretched across my face. After a few minutes of pleasantries, they told me they were looking at buying a house in my area. Then they asked if I would be interested in living there and taking care of it when they were on the road traveling. I told them yes, but to be honest, I never actually thought they would buy the house.

A couple of weeks went by before I spoke with them again. This time, they told me that they were flying in the following week to close on the house. They wanted to know if I would still be interested in taking care of it for them. They said that I could think about it and let them know when they arrived. When I finished the call I sat stunned in silence.

For the next several days I went over the pros and cons of the offer. It would mean I would have to commute fifty miles each way to work and would therefore cost me more in gas. However, the one thing that kept coming back to me was this: how could I pass up such a blessing? I could have said no to this amazing gift, but I couldn't bring myself to do it.

Every day I lived in that house, I knew the blessings of God when I woke up in the morning, and every night when I pulled into the garage I thanked Him that I lived where I did. Each time I watched the sunset from the deck or saw the stars that hung above, I knew it was all due to God. I accepted the amazement of what God had provided for me.

MANY TIMES WHEN GOD BLESSES US, IT COMES IN AN INSTANT AND IT IS UP TO US TO ACCEPT IT OR TO REJECT IT.

One of the most interesting aspects of the human spirit is tendency to resist it when something amazing happens. We seek and pray for a miracle, sometimes even for years, but as soon as we receive it we start looking for the strings attached. It reminds me of the Wizard of Oz. As most of you know, Dorothy, the Lion, the Tin Man, and Scarecrow finally made it to the wizard, and each received what they had asked for. However, in the end, the wizard is not really all that powerful after all. He is just a man behind a large illusion.

When God performs miracles in our lives, in the back of our minds we may wonder if the blessings are just illusions. We have been brought up in a culture that says that everything has a price, and that nothing in life is free. This view is continually reinforced everywhere we look. Recently, there was a television show who gave each of the audience members a "free" car. The one hook was that the audience had to pay for the taxes due on the cars. In an instant something free turned into something with strings attached. We tend to view everything with the suspicion that the same is true.

Have you ever received anything for absolutely nothing in return? Do such things exist? Many will say "yes" to both. They will then point to the presents we receive at Christmas or on a birthday. Some will go on to point out the salvation which they received when they came to know Christ. Without question, this is the most important gift anyone will ever receive, and most of us seem to lose sight of it over time. Our salvation is more than fire insurance; it is freedom from the death that sin brings to our soul on a daily basis.

IF THE CHILDREN OF ISRAEL HAD REJECTED THE BLESSINGS OF GOD, THEY WOULD NEVER HAVE REACHED THE PROMISE THAT GOD HAD FOR THEM.

Let me ask my previous question another way, have you ever received something so great you either would not accept it or you were hesitant to do so? When the gift was offered, did you try to find the hidden strings? If so, I can assure you that you are not alone. I know you have heard of the saying "If it looks too good to be true it is." I can tell you from my experience this is more often true than not. I must caution you though, not to allow this view to keep you from the amazement God. I almost did and looking back, I am thankful I was able to accept Gods amazing gift. If the children of Israel had rejected the blessings of God, they would never have reached the promise that God had for them. If they had questioned God's actions instead of accepting them, they would have never been free. Are we so different? Do we ever tell ourselves that the blessings from God look too good to be true? Have we ever accepted God's blessing on one hand, but then spent time worrying about when they will be taken away? How do we react when God offers us something that is simply amazing?

How do you treat the blessings God has given you, today? Have you accepted your salvation with amazement? Do you rejoice in your relationship with the Father? We have to realize that we are children of God, and by that very fact we are blessed. I urge you to make yourself learn the lesson I did, to simply accept the blessings of God with unabashed amazement.

ACCEPTING AMAZEMENT

Exodus 12:31-36

31 Then he called for Moses and Aaron by night, and said, "Rise, go out from among my people, both you and the children of Israel. And go, serve the LORD as you have said. 32 Also take your flocks and your herds, as you have said, and be gone; and bless me also." 33 And the Egyptians urged the people, that they might send them out of the land in haste. For they said, "We shall all be dead." 34 So the people took their dough before it was leavened, having their kneading bowls bound up in their clothes on their shoulders. 35 Now the children of Israel had done according to the word of Moses, and they had asked from the Egyptians articles of silver, articles of gold, and clothing. 36 And the LORD had given the people favor in the sight of the Egyptians, so that they granted them what they requested. Thus they plundered the Egyptians.

Review Questions:

1. Reading the story in Exodus 12, what are some of the amazing events that happened to the Children of Israel?

2. Is it hard for you to accept when something amazing happens in your life? Why do you believe it is hard for you to sometimes accept the wonderful gifts God gives you?

3. Instead of focusing on your life and what you deserve, where should you keep your focus? What are some small things that can be done daily to remind you to keep your priorities straight?

4. Who was the source of the favor that the Israelites received when they left Egypt? In what ways did they see that favor??

5. Look back on your life. What are some amazing things that have happened? Can you now see how God brought these things about?

Chapter 4
CHANGING COURSE NOT DESTINATION

A man's heart plans his way, But the Lord directs his step
Proverbs 16:9

It's always good to plot a course of action. However, it's just as vital that you learn how to change it from time to time. I was once told of an Admiral in the US Navy who learned this lesson the hard way.

Admiral James Howard III led his battalion of ships through dense fog on a cool April morning. Aboard his aircraft carrier, he had spent most of the night mapping out his course. According to his calculations, they would be in the next port by the time the sun set.

During his thirty years in the Navy, Howard had become a very proud sailor. He was convinced the battalion of ships he now commanded could stand up against anything on the high seas. There were even times he wished someone would challenge them so that he could prove it.

As he looked out from the bridge, all he could see was a blanket of fog that now engulfed the battle group. He could barely see beyond the edge of the aircraft carrier. In all his years of service, he had never seen fog so thick.

As he was scanned the horizon, trying to find a break in the fog, he thought he saw a faint light directly in front of him. His gaze froze on its location. Was his mind playing tricks on him, or did he indeed see a light?

It took a moment for him to grasp the reality. What could be producing a light directly in front of him? Surely there was not another ship out in this heavy fog! Debating with himself, he radioed the others ships to confirm what he saw. Yes, indeed, all the ships in the battle group reported back that they too saw a light coming through the fog. More disturbing still, they all believed the light was coming from a location directly in front of the aircraft carrier.

Soon the radio was alive with traffic. Then the aircraft carrier received a radio transmission that stood out from the rest. The message was simple: "To the commander of the ship that is sailing in our direction: change course to avoid collision."

The Admiral could not believe what he was hearing. He knew there was not a ship on the seas that could compare to the size or might of this carrier. How dare this intruder command them to change course?

The Admiral ordered his radio operator to respond. "We will not yield. It is YOU who must change course to avoid collision."

Moments later, the response came over the radio. "To the commander of the ship that is sailing in our direction: change course to avoid collision."

No one in his right mind could really think that an entire battalion of ships would move for him, the Admiral thought. He radioed back as the light continued to grow and the distance between them lessened. Still, the man on the other end did not change his response.

The Admiral's blood boiled. He'd had enough of this exchange. He took the headset in his hand, determined to make himself clear. He would not change course. In a burst of anger, he called out over the radio waves, "I am an Admiral of the US Navy and I am the commander of the aircraft carrier and the battalion of ships that are heading your direction. We have the might and power of the Unites States Armed Forces, and we are not going to change course. You must change course or you will be run over." As he finished, dead silence fell all around.

His anger could be seen on his face. His sailors knew that if the Admiral said something, then he would follow through with it. None of them knew what would happen next. They all hoped the man on the other end would back down. This was no time to play a game of chicken on the high seas.

It seemed like an eternity before the radio waves crackled again with life. The transmission was clear and to the point. *"This is John Moorhead, and I am the operator of this lighthouse."*

IT'S ALWAYS GOOD TO PLOT A COURSE OF ACTION. HOWEVER, IT'S JUST AS VITAL THAT YOU LEARN HOW TO CHANGE IT FROM TIME TO TIME.

Admiral James Howard III almost paid a great price for his unwillingness to change course. Instead of listening to the voice calling out to him, he allowed his pride to deafen him. Out of his pride came a voice, not of understanding or humility, but of arrogance and an unwillingness to accept that he did not know all the facts of the situation.

There are times in all of our lives we experience moments of fog. We have moments when our minds tell us to turn around, and other times where they tell us to stay on course. However, we are unable to see what lies ahead. It is in these moments that we must be willing to humble ourselves before God and admit we do not know what to do next. There will be times when God tells us to stay the course. Yet, there will also be times when He suggests another way. In these times, He will call us to change the direction we are heading, and we must listen.

Most of us enjoy consistency in life. All of us would rather sail on calm seas than on turbulent ones. So when change in life does arise, we usually choose to fight it instead of embrace it. Some people argue that we don't need to accept change, because God states in His word that He is the same yesterday, today, and forever. While there is truth in this argument, we must also remember that we are not God. The fact is life is filled with change. As we move through life, God continues to change the direction we thought we were traveling. God has often been referred to as the potter and humans as His clay. Does the clay tell the potter what steps He needs to take to make it into a bowl? When the potter's hands are working through the clay, does the clay respond that the potter is not doing it correctly? How then can we believe we can tell God the direction in which we are to go? How can we say yes to the destination He has for us and then tell Him we have a better way to get there?

AS WE MOVE THROUGH LIFE, GOD CONTINUES TO CHANGE THE DIRECTION WE THOUGHT WE WERE TRAVELING.

God has given us free will, and we are able to choose to follow His plan for our life or reject the destination He has for us. However, it is not good enough to accept the destination if we are unwilling to also accept the path He has chosen. There are many things between the the beginning of the journey until its end that we do not know, but God calls us to accept His calling anyway.

How then should we approach the journey? How do we get from the promise of God to the fulfillment of that promise? The truth is, the only way that we will reach the end is to follow His path. The thought that the destination can be reached any other way is a lie that the enemy wants you to believe.

So how do you know when and where you must change direction? This question can only be answered by hearing God's voice. Do you worry that you can't hear His voice? God has created all of us, and He has promised to send His spirit to be our comfort and counselor. By placing His Spirit within us, He has also placed within all of us His voice. Jesus said that His sheep would know His voice (John 10:27). His voice is the one that calls out to us when we are surrounded by the fog of life. His voice brings peace and love. All He needs from you is a listening ear. Will you be willing to listen when He calls, or will you be bound and determined to stay on your own course? You might want to think long and hard before you respond. The answer that you give may mean the difference between a collision and safe passage to your final destination.

CHANGING COURSE NOT DESTINATION

Exodus 13:17 (KJV)

17 Then it came to pass, when Pharaoh had let the people go, that God did not lead them by way of the land of the Philistines, although that was near; for God said, "Lest perhaps the people change their minds when they see war, and return to Egypt."

Review Questions:

1. Do you know what direction you are heading?

____
____
____
____
____

2. Have you stopped to spend time with God to ensure that you are heading in the right direction? If so, are you heading in the direction God wants you to go?

____
____
____
____
____

3. Are you prepared to lay anything and everything aside if God asked?

____
____
____

4. If you are not heading in the right direction, what are some things that you could begin doing today to turn yourself around? (Ex. Prayer, spending time in the word, spending time with God, etc.)

____
____
____
____
____

Chapter 5

RED LIGHT - GREEN LIGHT

Then he said to Him, "If Your Presence does not go with us, do not bring us up from here."
Exodus 33:15

The cloud on the valley floor followed the sun as it rose in the east. The pillar of gray and white swirled against the horizon, rising higher and higher. This sight had become as common as the sunrise every morning.

Alon gathered his belongings and rolled up his tent. As he got his things together, he could not stop looking at the cloud that now moved high above. His tribe had followed this cloud for so long, it was hard for him to remember what life had been like before.

The cloud that Alon and his people followed was not an ordinary cloud by any means. It rose each morning with the sun. Then, as the sun set, it would transform into a pillar of fire. Some days the cloud would move great distances. At other times, the cloud or the pillar of fire would remain in place for many days or weeks.

Thinking back to what now seemed the distant past, Alon recalled the first day the cloud had appeared. He had heard the voice of Moses telling them that God would go with them. The LORD Himself would tell them when and where to move. As a visual sign of God's presence, the cloud appeared. Moses declared that the cloud would guide them in the day, and at night would become a pillar of fire. The pillar of fire would watch over them and guard them from their enemies.

Since that moment, Alon had known that his leader had a close relationship with their God. Each time Moses said something, it came to pass. At first, Alon had more faith in Moses' words than in the God he spoke for. However, his faith in God grew with the passing of time.

AS ISRAEL FOLLOWED GOD TO THE PROMISED LAND, THEY WENT UNDER HIS PROTECTION. WHEN HE MOVED, THEY MOVED. WHEN HE STOOD STILL, THEY DID THE SAME.

The God his leader served was now also the God Alon served. With trust and obedience, he followed the cloud that moved before him. It represented a protection that stood over his people. As long as they followed it, he knew God was with him. He could not explain why or how he knew, but deep within him he found peace in this knowledge.

Alon's tribe was known as the tribe of Asher, one of the twelve tribes of Israel. As Israel followed God to the Promised Land, they went under His protection. When He moved, they moved. When He stood still, they did the same. Looking into the past, we see that it was by following God's plan that Israel came to possess the promise.

I can best relate this principle to a game I played when I was a child. Growing up in the 80's, we spent most of our time playing games outside with neighborhood kids. Instead of video games, we played games that we made up as we went along. Other games, I imagine, were played by children everywhere. One game was called"Red Light, Green Light."

The object was simple. Now, as I look back, I wonder how we had so much fun with such a simplistic game. As a group, we would line up on one side of the street while one kid stood on the other side. When that one kid said "green light," we would walk as fast as we could across the street. When he or she said "red light," we would stop in our tracks. This would continue until someone made it to the other side and was declared the winner.

As we follow the path to God's promise, we have to apply the principles of this game to our lives. When God says "green light," we need to be moving. However, the moment that He says "red light" we must stop. I remember as a child that it was hard to stop because my desire to get to the other side was so great. In life we struggle with the same problem. Most of us are okay with the "green lights" of life, but have a hard time with the "red lights."

As the Children of Israel undertook their journey to the Promised Land, they did so with the direction and guidance of God. As they woke in the morning, they looked to God to tell them to stay or to move. When God was on the move, the people were there on His heels. When God stopped, the people set up camp and stayed in that location until God moved again. They did not strike out in front of Him, nor did they linger in an area once God had departed.

It is vital that we adopt the same attitude as we move toward the promise that God has given us. We have to be willing to give up control of our direction and the speed at which we travel.

In this day and age, this second part can prove to be more difficult than the first. We live in a time of instant gratification, and the principle of waiting is a thing of the past. We have instant oatmeal, microwave meals, fast food, on-demand movies, instant messaging, emails, and cell phones. The goal of most of our new inventions is to get something—anything--faster and easier.

While I must admit that I love most of the new technology available today (and I own a number of "instant" devices), waiting is overall a positive thing. Waiting brings reflection and preparation. Most of the time it allows us to step back and examine a situation from all sides. From this vantage point, we can not only take the next step, but do so with the confidence that it is the best step.

Do you remember a time that you blindly ran into something?

I do, and looking back I can say that though my heart was in it, God was not. I met a girl and we began the normal dating routine. We went out on dates and spent hours talking on the phone, laughing, joking, and getting to know one another. It seemed that the more time we spent with each other, the more we fit. Our relationship took off like a Roman candle on the 4th of July. I was open to hearing God's "green lights," but when He said "red light" I chose not to listen.

IF WE CHOOSE TO STAY WHEN HE SAYS GO, OR TO GO WHEN HE SAYS STAY, WE WILL BE IN REBELLION.

Like a Roman candle, our relationship started out with fire, sparks, beautiful color, and vibrant life. However, again much like a candle, it was short lived. Six weeks into this "magical relationship" everything fell apart. Looking back on the experience, I know that if I had listened to God's voice instead of my own desires I would have heard Him call "red light." Failing to hear His call resulted in undue stress and hardship for both of us.

As humans, we make mistakes. There may be times when we fail to hear God's voice. We must open our hearts and minds to accepting His direction. There will be times that He tells us to dive in, and we must be willing to do so. However, we must also be willing to stop in our tracks if that is His will. If we choose to stay when He says go, or to go when He says stay, we will be in rebellion. Do you trust God enough to be willing to keep pace with Him?

RED LIGHT - GREEN LIGHT

Exodus 13:21 - 14:1

21 And the LORD went before them by day in a pillar of cloud to lead the way, and by night in a pillar of fire to give them light, so as to go by day and night. 22 He did not take away the pillar of cloud by day or the pillar of fire by night from before the people.

Review Questions:

1. Do you remember a time when God told you to go and instead you chose to stay?

2. Are you sitting back and waiting on your promise to come to you, or are you getting up and moving toward it?

3. Are you willing to break out of your daily routine to see your promise fulfilled?

Chapter 6
WORRYWARTS ARE NOT CAUSED BY FROGS

Trust in Him at all times, you people; Pour out your heart before Him;
God is a refuge for us.
Psalms 62:8

As a young boy growing up, I spent a lot of time outside. I would ride my bike, play war, and yes, even play with frogs. I remember an old wives' tale that said "If you play with frogs then you will get warts." As a kid, I never really worried about such things; however, when I saw someone with a wart, I would always think, "They must have been playing with frogs."

As I grew up, I learned the truth: warts are not from frogs at all. They are actually caused by a virus in the body, and while a wart may be annoying, it does not mean the end of the world. I have also learned that warts are not contained to someone's physical body. They can also attach themselves to a person's spiritual life.

The warts that infest your spiritual life are known as worrywarts, and they are directly related to how you handle FROGS. When I speak of FROGS, I am not speaking about the small green animals that are found on your lawn. In your spiritual life, FROGS stands for Fully Relying On God's Sovereignty.

So how do you know if you have worrywarts? There are both seen and unseen signs that will let you know. Let me list just a few:

1) **A lack of peace (or a feeling of uneasiness)**
2) **Stress--both mental and physical**
3) **Lack of sleep**
4) **Worry (sometimes masked as "concern")**
5) **Doubt**
6) **Fear**
7) **Depression or a feeling of hopelessness**

If you have any of these symptoms, what can you do? Is there anything that you can do to rid your life of worrywarts?

As most of you know, getting rid of warts on your physical body is as simple as covering them with a solution you can buy at any drug store. You may even freeze them off, however the concept is the same. You attack them with a concentration of a solution you know will work. How do you know the solution will work? Because you have seen it work for others, or you have experienced it working in your own life.

IN YOUR SPIRITUAL LIFE,
FROGS STANDS FOR FULLY RELYING ON
GOD'S SOVEREIGNTY.

Worrywarts of the soul may not be visible, but you remove them the same way. You find a solution that works and you aggressively attack them. The root cause of all worrywarts is a lack of faith in God's ability. Fear, doubt, and many other things are only the symptoms of this root cause.

If the root cause of worrywarts is the lack of faith in God's ability, then the solution is in Fully Relying On God's Sovereignty. Let's take a closer look at what this means.

Fully – aggressively with all that you have

Relying – completely depending on, without reservation or hesitation

On – not beside or with, but actually standing "on" the word of God

God's – this means on His power and not our own

Sovereignty – His complete control and ability to handle everything and anything in life

I would love to say that getting rid of worrywarts is as easy as getting rid of physical warts; the truth is it is not. If you want to get rid of worry, then it will take effort, time, and the ability to give up control.

This may sound pretty simple, but the fact is that our flesh hates to give up control. In order to get your flesh to yield, you must strengthen your spirit. You can only be led by one, the spirit or flesh, and you alone must decide which one it will be.

How do you strengthen your spirit?

Begin by surrendering everything in your life to God. This will require you to physically say the words of surrender out loud, because in the kingdom of God spoken words are important. God Himself spoke the universe into existence, and it continues to expand. God told us in His word that every word from His mouth will go forth and will not come back void. In your mouth and on your tongue lie the power of life and death. Begin by confessing your inadequacies to God, and then surrender everything to Him.

Once you have spilled your life out before God, you need to pause and listen. God does and will speak; however, at this point, it is also important to just spend time in His presence. No one can be in the presence of God and not be changed.

The hardest part of this process is in this: when God does speak, He may ask you to give up something you hold very dear. Why? The answer is because He does not want us to have anything in our lives that we love more than Him. He alone is the source of all things on Earth. How then do we find ourselves loving the things of life more than the Creator of all things?

Some will be unwilling to lay everything down, while others will choose to lay only portions of their lives before God. This is like renting a house from someone and only allowing the landlord to access certain parts of it to make repairs. It is the owner's responsibility to repair and keep up the physical structure of the house. If you do not allow him access to the whole house, how can he improve the conditions in which you live?

NO ONE CAN BE IN THE PRESENCE OF GOD AND NOT BE CHANGED.

Many people will not let God come into certain rooms of their hearts because they know that things are not in the order in which He created them. When they do allow God in, they try to make excuses as to why their hearts look the way they do. This may be a way to defend yourself against a landlord, but God already knows the condition of our hearts.

Once we let Him in, He does not condemn us. Instead, He restores us and improves our lives.

The next step that must be taken, once you have laid everything before the Lord, is to get up and leave your worries behind. This is harder than it sounds because our flesh will not willingly give up control. God gives us instructions on how to fight this problem. He tells us to take every thought captive and place it under the blood of Christ. It is only through His blood that we can become victorious in the battle of our minds.

When you do stumble and fall, how do you respond? Do you make excuses and blame your flesh? Do you throw in the towel and give up striving to do right? The reason I ask is because there will be times in your life when you miss the mark. It is very important to remember the difference between a conqueror in Christ and a defeated warrior. The conqueror gets back up. When you are knocked down by the hardships of life, do you stay down or get back up? Do you withdraw into yourself, or do you fall to your knees before God and seek Him? The way that you answer the above questions will tell you if you are on the road to worrywarts or if you are Fully Relying On God's Sovereignty.

I once thought myself on top of the world, self-reliant and in charge of every part of my life. I was in college, popular, and had everything I could have dreamed of. All I saw in front of me was a world of promise and possibilities with nothing in my way. That's when the bottom fell out of the world I had created by the work of my hands.

My grades were failing. I went from graduating in the top ten of my high school to being on academic probation. The social life I lived for was torn from end to end. I could not believe I had fallen so far so fast, and when I hit bottom, I did so with full force.

I remember sitting on the floor in my room with my knees tucked up against my chest, crying out to God. I had grown up in a Christian home and had been saved when I was twelve years old. I had been active in the youth group and in many good organizations through my high school years. However, in those years I was seeking what was good to me, and not what was good to God.

GOD DOES NOT CONDEMN US WHEN WE FALL. IT IS IN OUR WEAKNESS THAT HIS POWER IS THE MOST APPARENT.

While I was running my life without God, He did not forget me, nor did He leave me to my own devices. I would go to church on Sundays, and on occasion He would even speak to me. I thought I could give God part of my life and that would be enough. The truth is He wanted much more. The sad fact is that, until my world fell apart, I was unwilling to give it to Him.

Once everything came crumbling down, I surrendered my whole life to Him. In the next few years, I saw my life change. He changed my perspective, my thoughts, my desires, and even my friends. My desires were taken away and replaced by God's desires for me. Along the way I have fallen, but each time God has been faithful. When I was knocked down, His hand was there helping me back up.

God does not condemn us when we fall. It is in our weakness that His power is the most apparent. These times in our lives cause us to refocus our attention on Him. In these moments, we realize that He alone is the source for all things in life. Growing pains come with growth, because we must leave parts of ourselves behind in order to grow into the life God has for us.

The truth remains that until you can Fully Rely On God's Sovereignty and let go of your own ways, you will never get rid of the worrywarts in your life. Failing to solve this problem up front will keep you from enjoying your promise once it comes to pass. Always remember, freedom, not warts, comes from FROGS.

WORRYWARTS ARE NOT CAUSED BY FROGS

Exodus 14:13-14

13 And Moses said to the people, "Do not be afraid. Stand still, and see the salvation of the LORD, which He will accomplish for you today. For the Egyptians whom you see today, you shall see again no more forever. 14
"The LORD will fight for you, and you shall hold your peace."

Exodus 20:20

20 And Moses said to the people, "Do not fear; for God has come to test you, and that His fear may be before you, so that you may not sin."

Numbers 14:9

9 Only do not rebel against the LORD. And do not be afraid of the people of the land, because we will swallow them up. Their protection is gone, but the LORD is with us. Do not be afraid of them."

Deuteronomy 31:6

6 "Be strong and of good courage, do not fear nor be afraid of them; for the LORD your God, He is the One who goes with you. He will not leave you nor forsake you."

Review Questions:

1. What are you worried about?

____

____

____

____

____

2. Reflecting on the Scriptures above, how can you reconcile your worries with God's reassurance?

____

____

____

____

____

3. What does it mean to Fully Rely on God's Sovereignty?

4. What are some steps that you can take today to begin Fully Relying on God's Sovereignty?

5. What does God promise to give you once you begin to fully rely on Him?

Chapter 7

WHY WAIT?

Wait for the LORD and keep his way. He will exalt you to inherit the land; when the wicked are cut off, you will see it.
Psalm 37:34 NIV

Whispers traveled through the camp. Where had their leader gone? The people were getting more nervous with each passing day. It was hard to believe that a month had passed since they had arrived at this mountain. By all accounts, they were nomads, a people without a home. They had been traveling for some time; this was their longest rest since their journey began.

Along the way they had seen many wild and unimaginable things. Miracle after miracle followed them. There had been several times when all hope seemed lost and death was all but certain. Yet, each time their leader, Moses, had assured them that they would be delivered--and each time, they were.

Their leader was strange and peculiar. He spent several hours alone every day praying and seeking wisdom from his God. The concept of a higher power was not foreign to the people of the camp. They had seen many gods in the land they came from. Some of the gods looked like jackals, others like snakes, and others like lions. Each god was responsible for some part of life, from the rising of the sun to the changing of the seasons, and each were worshiped accordingly.

What made Moses' God so interesting was that no one had seen Him. They had seen His power, but they had never actually seen Him. What was even more unusual was that He was the only God Moses believed in. He was a God who was over all and responsible for all. This was such a strange concept to some in the camp that it was hard for them to grasp. Moses had asked them to put aside all of their previous experiences and take up the truth he was now showing them. Some accepted readily, but others resisted this change.

The most powerful thing Moses had brought them was hope. Hope for a new life, a new land, and most of all, freedom. It was with these promises that the two million plus people in the camp now followed Moses. They were going to a land of plenty, and they clung to this hope with all their might. Knowing their destination helped them to accept the long journey that would take them there.

However, they had failed to count on the many trials they would encounter along the way. Neither had they counted on sitting at the base of a mountain for over a month without a leader. So where was Moses? The last time he had spoken to them, he was going up to speak with his God. He had left his brother in charge and had only taken his apprentice with him. Since then, several weeks had passed and there was no sign of his return.

Like the wind, rumors and speculations now flew through the camp. Some said he had left them to go back to his home. Others said he must have died on the climb and he would never be coming back. Only a handful kept the faith, and, their numbers dwindled with each passing day.

Most looked to Moses' brother, Aaron, for answers, but each time they asked his response was the same: "I do not know." Aaron was left fielding the questions about his brother's whereabouts that came with greater frequency and vehemence every day. The camp grew restless. They wanted to be on the move. The promise of a new home and a land of plenty filled their hearts and dreams.

Suddenly, the flood of doubts and worries overflowed the banks of reason and swept up everyone in its path. Like dominoes falling, one person after another was caught up in this wave of insecurity. They were searching for something or someone to be grounded on. The wave of people crashed upon the doorstep of a reluctant Aaron, who felt acutely that he had been left behind to guard the uncontrollable.

The people demanded to know the whereabouts of their leader and his God. They wanted to see his God for themselves. Where was the god that promised them freedom? Where was the god that performed miracles? In Egypt, when things were not going well, the people would make sacrifices to their gods to appease them. The people brought their argument to Aaron: if they had gods to sacrifice to, then they would be delivered to the land of plenty. They demanded that gods be made for them..

Like a sandcastle built upon a stormy beach, Aaron crumbled under the tide. His will, devotion, and loyalty were washed away by his fear of the people that now stood before him. As his fortitude gave way, he ordered all the gold of the camp to be brought forth. From it, he would make them a god to worship.

The piles grew all day as the people tossed necklaces, bracelets, and gold cups into them. Each family gladly gave up their treasure for a part in this great undertaking. They gave no thought to the laws that Moses' God had given them when they first came to this mountain, commanding them to make no graven image and worship no other gods. In a matter of hours, a decision had been made and the wheels of disobedience put into motion. Now it seemed that nothing could stop the entire camp from falling over the cliff of betrayal.

As quickly as the piles grew, the gold was taken to the fire pits. There, channels were built and red hot coals stoked. The raging flames of the fire consumed the gold, turning it into a hot yellowish liquid. Gravity pulled the liquid gold down through the channels into a mold below. The artists of the camp had carved the mold days before. They could not wait until their masterpiece was seen by all in the camp.

Once the mold was completely filled, the caps were put into place. Like a caterpillar within a cocoon, the liquid gold began to transform into a new creature. With each passing day the people of the camp grew more and more restless. They wanted to see what they had created, and their patience was running thin.

The day of the unveiling finally dawned. With the sound of beating drums, the dedication ceremony began. The artists stood by with chisels and hammers in the hands. With the striking of the drums they all raised their hammers and struck their chisels at the same time. The artists struck the form over and over again, their blows in sync with the beat of the drums. The wood that had served as a mold splintered off piece by piece until it was completely removed.

Silence fell on the crowd as they beheld the creation that now stood before them. Rays of sunlight reflected off the gold as if the light came from within the image itself. As the crowd drank in the image of a flawless golden calf, Aaron stood forth and raised his arms high in the sky.

"This is your god! This is the god that has delivered you from your enemy! This is the god that will lead you into the Promise Land."

When the last words of Moses' brother fell on the ears of the people, they erupted into cheers. The sound was deafening, echoing through the valley. With those words, the golden calf they had all helped create now became the very god they worshiped.

INSTEAD OF WAITING FOR GOD TO DELIVER THEIR PROMISE TO THEM, THE CHILDREN OF ISRAEL TURNED TO THE GOD OF SELF.

The people broke out into dancing and singing. They bowed and worship before the calf. They threw presents before it and sacrificed to it. All of these things the people gave to a god they had formed with their own hands, blind to the truth that the beautiful golden calf was without life or power.

The noise from the celebration rose high in the air and the sounds flowed up the mountain. Moses' apprentice had been waiting for his master when he heard the noise from below. He turned and began to race toward the place where he had last seen Moses, intending to carry the news to him. As he did, he saw Moses emerge from a thick cloud of smoke, carrying two tablets of stone engraved with the Law of God.

"Master, there is war in the camp below, can you not hear it?"

Soon the apprentice was following along behind Moses as they hurried down to the camp. Finally, they emerged from the fog and had a clear view of what was happening below. They were both overcome with shock and horror as they realized what their eyes beheld. There was no war, no army attacking, no one running for their lives. What the two beheld was much worse.

There before them was Aaron, Moses' own brother, dressed in gold and silver. His arms stretched high above his head as he offered sacrifices to a golden calf. Anger rose deep within Moses, and with all of his might he threw the tablets of stone through the air. The sound of the stone smashing against the mountain was deafening. Instantly the music below stopped as all eyes searched to find the source of the disturbance.

At that moment Moses shouted out, and the world the Israelites and Aaron had built for themselves came crashing down around them. The camp had made a choice to look to a man-made god for guidance instead of looking to the true God. Their mistake was fatal. That day 3000 men lost their lives because the Israelites had chosen to take matters into their own hands.

Aaron, Moses brother, led the children of Israel whenever Moses left to spend time with God. Aaron had stood next to Moses from the time of his brother's return to Egypt. He had witnessed the plagues, the parting of the Red Sea, and God's miraculous providence throughout their journey. Why then did Aaron allow the people to pressure him into making an idol for them to worship?

Little by little, day by day, the people had chipped away at Aaron's fortitude. Slowly, he became more and more tolerant of the ideas of the people around him, until he finally gave them what they wanted. He orchestrated the creation of the calf, and when it was finished he presented it to the people and proclaimed that this was the god who had delivered them.

The seed of betrayal had been planted within Aaron's heart, and with each decision he made, it grew. Aaron betrayed his brother's trust by leading the people away from God. He betrayed the people by not standing for the truth that he knew within his heart. His ultimate betrayal, though, was against God. When Aaron pronounced that the golden calf was god, he betrayed the true God that had led the children of Israel out of Egypt. That day, he and the children of Israel chose to trade the God of the universe for the gold in their hands.

Instead of waiting for God to deliver their promise to them, the children of Israel turned to the god of self. With their own hands they created the answer they wanted. Have you ever chosen to look to someone or something other than God for guidance in your life? I hope that none of us has built a golden calf to worship, but I would dare say that all of us, at some time, have chosen to find our own way instead of waiting on God. This could mean something as simple as trusting a person, a job, or material possessions to help you, instead of waiting for God.

Are you willing to jeopardize your promise because you are unwilling to wait on God?

WHY WAIT?

Exodus 32:1-6

Now when the people saw that Moses delayed coming down from the mountain, the people gathered together to Aaron, and said to him, "Come, make us gods that shall go before us; for as for this Moses, the man who brought us up out of the land of Egypt, we do not know what has become of him." 2
And Aaron said to them, "Break off the golden earrings which are in the ears of your wives, your sons, and your daughters, and bring them to me."
3 "So all the people broke off the golden earrings which were in their ears,
and brought them to Aaron. 4 And he received the gold from their hand, and he fashioned it with an engraving tool, and made a molded calf. Then they said, "This is your god, O Israel, that brought you out of the land of Egypt!"
5 So when Aaron saw it, he built an altar before it. And Aaron made a proclamation and said, "Tomorrow is a feast to the LORD." 6 Then they
rose early on the next day, offered burnt offerings, and brought peace offerings; and the people sat down to eat and drink, and rose up to play.

Review Questions:

1. What was the price Israel paid for not waiting on the Lord?

____

____

____

____

____

2. Are you living off of God's provision and trusting Him, or are you trying to live off of what you can produce with your own hands and find the way for yourself?

____

____

____

____

____

3. Are there times that you have felt forgotten by God?

____

____

____

4. On some level do you believe that God owes you the fulfillment of the promise, because you have waited so long?

5. How long are you willing to wait for your promise to come true?

Chapter 8

DEFEATING DISTRACTIONS

It was not by their sword that they won the land, nor did their arm bring them victory; it was your right hand, your arm, and the light of your face, for you loved them
Psalm 44:3 NIV

"Hurry, they have returned!" The speaker and his friends ran to the center of the camp, where all the people had gathered, crowding around the twelve men who had just returned. The crowd pushed forward as each person tried to hear better the tale of their adventures.

The twelve were not ordinary men by any account, nor was the journey they had just finished an everyday one. The men represented each of the twelve tribes of Israel. They had been sent out to scout the land that had been promised to them. After a long and intensive search, they had returned to tell the people of everything they had found.

There was another man standing among the twelve, and all seemed to be focused on him. Moses had grown old since the exodus from Egypt. He leaned on a large staff in his right hand. He raised the staff high in the air and signaled to the crowd to be silent.

As the noise of the crowd dissipated, the scouts stepped back and reveled what they had been hiding. Behind them were the largest grapes, dates, and other fruits that any one in the crowd had ever seen. The bounty that lay before the people stirred the emotions of the crowd, and with great joy they began to raise their voices again.

Soon the noise of jubilation was almost deafening. Yet, ten of the twelve remained quite and solemn, unaffected by the crowd's enthusiasm. Among themselves, the twelve prodded and argued until at last one turned and faced the crowd. He waved his arms, trying fervently to quiet the crowd. It took some time, but the crowd finally understood this man had something very important to say. They fell silent.

The man's face showed none of the joy that the people expected. Instead, he seemed afraid—not of the crowd, or of his fellow scouts, but of the tale he had to tell.

He began to weave his tale, telling the people how he and his partner had secretly entered into the land that lay over the mountains. They descended upon the villages below and were overwhelmed with the goodness that lay there. The fruit was larger, the fields greener, the water sweeter than they could have imagined—the land was rich beyond their wildest dreams. After scouting for a day the two, they came upon their first city. They had hidden outside its high gates and waited to get a glimpse of its inhabitants.

That evening they took turns sleeping and keeping watch. When the sun rose the next day, the two watched as its rays fell softly on the mountainside. As they watched the sunrise, they heard a sudden sound from the gates. They turned to see the huge doors of the city open wide. Once the gates were pulled apart, the people came out from the city to work the land.

The people of this land stood many feet taller than anyone they had ever seen. The weapons they carried were longer and more lethal than anything the scouts possessed. As the crowd listened, spellbound, the scout recalled looking at the giants as fear began to overtake his heart and mind. Just days before, he and his companion were celebrating the goodness of the land. Now they only wished to escape it. A change came over him even as he told the story, as he grew white and shook with remembered fear.

As the man finished his tale, a deathly silence fell on all those around. Then another scout came forth and poured out what his eyes had seen. Like the first, his tale began with joy in the goodness of the land, but soon it too turned to the people that possessed it.

This scout focused on the cities and how tall the walls were, how wide, how impenetrable. As he finished his tale, the others came forth one by one until ten of the twelve men had spoken. All of their stories began with joy and ended in terror.

Two of the twelve stayed back, shaking their heads. Yes, indeed, they had seen the things that the other ten saw. They too had eaten of the goodness of the land, and they had approached the cities. In their reports they too noted the fortifications and the might of the cities and people. Yet, they also knew they had been given this land as a promise, not by man, but by the one true God.

When the twelve were sent out, they were told to find the best way to enter the land. They were not told to judge whether or not to enter--only to determine the best way to do so. Ten of the twelve seemed to have forgotten the mission, and instead became focused on the people and fortifications of the land. Instead of staying on task, they chose to see all of the things that would keep them from inhabiting the Promised Land.

OUTWARDLY THEY WERE DISTRACTED BY THE SIZE OF THE BARRIERS THAT LAY BETWEEN THEM AND THE PROMISE.

The final two scouts could no longer contain themselves. They burst forward with a story of their own to tell. They spoke of the large cites and overwhelming people, however, only for a moment. Most of their time was spent on the goodness of the land. Finally, they turned their attention to the resources that had been given to them. They tried in vain to draw the crowd's attention back to the promise and to the Promise-Giver.

No matter what they said, they could see that it was already too late. The words of poison the ten had poured out had entered the people's hearts and killed the hope they had carried for so many years. As the stories sunk in, a new sound began to rise in the camp. The people cried out in fear and anguish until all sounds of faith were drowned out. Moses finally gave way under the pressure and made the decision not to enter the land.

That day the two scouts, Joshua and Caleb, stood by the promise that was given to them by God. They stayed focused on the goal and refused to be dissuaded by what their eyes beheld. This stance almost cost them their lives as the people of the camp became angry with them; however, they were determined to stay the course. The other ten spies and the whole assembly of Israelites could not see the promise because they became distracted, both inward and outwardly.

Outwardly they were distracted by the size of the barriers that lay between them and the promise. They saw the people, the cities, and the weapons, and they compared all of these things to the things they could see in their own camp. Inwardly, fear and doubt had finally killed the faith and hope that they had carried out of Egypt.

Through Israel's response that day, we see that distractions can keep us from our promise. However, we also see that allowing distractions in life to deter us is an individual choice. Each spy saw and experienced the same things, yet ten concluded one thing and two another. Ten of the spies spoke out of fear; only two spoke out of faith.

Can distractions affect our ability to receive our promises from God? When was the last time you were distracted? For most of us, daily life is filled with distractions. Even now, as you read these words, you may be dealing with a distraction. Have you ever been distracted when your spouse or a family member was speaking to you? Have you ever been so nervous that you could not concentrate on what you were doing? Distractions come in two forms, inward and outward, but both keep us from completing the task at hand.

DISTRACTIONS CAN KEEP US FROM OUR PROMISE

We are living in the information age where multitasking is seen as a must. With the new gadgets and toys, it seems that everyone is trying to cope with sensory overload. It has become that much easier to be overwhelmed with distractions. One invention that has been around many years is the car radio. I love being able to drive down the road as I listen to my favorite song on my car stereo. However, I remember when doing so ended up costing me more than I would have liked.

At the time, I drove a Pontiac Grand Am. I had just gotten out of a college class and was driving home. The sun was shining and its warm rays fell through my open window. To be honest, I can't remember what song was playing. What I do remember is that I was oblivious to everything around me.

As I cruised along, I looked up and saw flashing lights behind me. I thought the police officer wanted by, so I moved over to the right lane, expecting him to pass me. I had done nothing wrong, and it never dawned on me that he wanted me to pull over.

I soon realized that I was wrong when he too pulled over into the right lane. Once I realized that he indeed wanted me to stop, I pulled into the next parking lot. The officer walked to my window and I looked at him with a puzzled look on my face. "Can I help you?" I asked.

Well, this took him by surprise. "Son," he said, "don't you know why I stopped you?" When I answered "no," he went on to tell me that I was going ten miles over the speed limit. I couldn't believe it! I told the officer that I was just heading home and listening to the radio. He believed me when I told him that I did not realize I was driving over the speed limit, but I still received a ticket.

Needless to say, the ticket cost me more than I wanted to pay, but I had broken the law and had to pay the price. I had allowed the distractions of the wonderful spring day, the feel of driving, and the song on the radio to distract me from how fast I was going. That day I learned a real lesson about outward distractions, however, I still had much to learn about inward distractions.

What do I mean by inward distractions? Inward distractions are those thoughts that bombard our minds and keep us from moving closer to our promise. The longer we spend trying to figure out how to make the promise come to pass, the longer it will take to happen.

SPENDING TIME ON THE "WHAT IF" ONLY SERVES TO TAKE YOU AWAY FROM THE VERY PURPOSE GOD HAS FOR YOU, JUST AS YOU ARE, RIGHT WHERE YOU ARE.

The most common inward distractions are fears, doubt, worries, and stress. When our mind is more focused on the situation we are in than on the promise God has given us, we are unable to keep our focus on our destination. Many people spend undue time trying to solve the "what if" problems in their lives. Spending time on the "what if" only serves to take you away from the very purpose God has for you, just as you are, right where you are.

We have all been created to worship, serve, and commune with God. When we start worrying about how we are going to make our promise a reality, what we are doing is actually taking our eyes off of God and putting them on ourselves. Our focus shifts from upward to inward, and regardless of what the New Age movement says, the fulfillment of our promise can only be found in God.

Let me give you a few examples of inward distractions. Have you ever been in church and spent most of the time thinking about other things? You try to sing the songs, but the only thing that you can think about is what you have to do when you get home. During your prayer time do you often find your thoughts drifting to other subjects? Do you hear the little voice inside telling you that you can't reach the destination God has set for you? All of these are just a few examples of inward distractions.

There are many passages of scripture that speak to this, but none better than Numbers chapter 13, which relates the story at the base of this chapter. Here we see the children of Israel on the brink of the promise that God has given them. They have waited, struggled, and endured for generations to see this come to pass. How did they handle the inward and outward distractions that faced them? What was the outcome of their reaction to the distractions? They failed to enter God's promise because they simply did not follow through. Instead of overcoming by faith, they were conquered by fear.

In life it is not the situation, but how we react to the situation, that will determine the outcome. Will you close your eyes and lift your voice to praise or will you turn inward and search for answers? These are important questions to ask before the situations come. If you are not already ready for the battle, you will be overrun in the chaos of the moment. The mind has often been referred to as a battleground. It is not a new concept, but it is a vital one for us to understand.

The Bible states that all the battles of our lives have already been won by the blood of Christ. Victory is assured. However, if we do not allow God to prepare us for battle, we will be left cowering in fear. The promise has been given by God. Therefore, we must stand firm and give praise to God in times of trial. Just as the darkest hour of the night is just before dawn, so it is in our spiritual lives. Fear will always attack and try to keep you from receiving your breakthrough. In those moments, it is crucial to press in to God.

**IN LIFE IT IS NOT THE SITUATION,
BUT HOW WE REACT TO THE SITUATION,
THAT WILL DETERMINE THE OUTCOME.**

We must all choose on a daily basis to live by faith or in fear. I encourage you to choose God, no matter what your thoughts tell you. God is always faithful to those who have faith in Him. Every word and every promise that proceeds from His mouth will come to pass. The question is, will you allow distractions to keep you from seeing them come to pass?

DEFEATING DISTRACTIONS

Numbers 13:26-33

26 Now they departed and came back to Moses and Aaron and all the congregation of the children of Israel in the Wilderness of Paran, at Kadesh; they brought back word to them and to all the congregation, and showed them the fruit of the land. 27 Then they told him, and said: "We went to the land where you sent us. It truly flows with milk and honey, and this is its fruit. 28 "Nevertheless the people who dwell in the land are strong; the cities are fortified and very large; moreover we saw the descendants of Anak there. 29 "The Amalekites dwell in the land of the South; the Hittites, the Jebusites, and the Amorites dwell in the mountains; and the Canaanites dwell by the sea and along the banks of the Jordan." 30 Then Caleb quieted the people before Moses, and said, "Let us go up at once and take possession, for we are well able to overcome it." 31 But the men who had gone up with him said, "We are not able to go up against the people, for they are stronger than we." 32 And they gave the children of Israel a bad report of the land which they had spied out, saying, "The land through which we have gone as spies is a land that devours its inhabitants, and all the people whom we saw in it are men of great stature. 33 "There we saw the giants (the descendants of Anak came from the giants); and we were like grasshoppers in our own sight, and so we were in their sight."

Numbers 14:1-4

1 So all the congregation lifted up their voices and cried, and the people wept that night. 2 And all the children of Israel complained against Moses and Aaron, and the whole congregation said to them, "If only we had died in the land of Egypt! Or if only we had died in this wilderness! 3 "Why has the LORD brought us to this land to fall by the sword, that our wives and children should become victims? Would it not be better for us to return to Egypt?" 4 So they said to one another, "Let us select a leader and return to Egypt."

Review Questions:

1. What are five distractions in your daily life?

2. How many times a week do you spend time in silence before God?

3. What are some ways that you can reduce the distractions in your life?

4. What separated Caleb and Joshua from the crowd? What was their reward for their choice?

Chapter 9

WHEN GOD SAYS "NO"

17 But from everlasting to everlasting the LORD's love is with those who fear him, and his righteousness with their children's children- 18 with those who keep his covenant and remember to obey his precepts.
Psalm 103:17-18

Nathan tried in vain to sit still as his wife attended to his wounds. The pain that shot through him was unbearable. His head swaggered back and forth as he fought to stay conscious. The battle was soon lost, and his body fell limp upon the ground. His wife screamed in panic as she fell upon him, trembling in tears.

Her head rested on his chest and she breathed a sigh of relief. By the slow rise and fall of his chest she knew that he was hanging on to life, if only by a string. Quickly, he was moved into a nearby tent. With a wet cloth his wife wiped his forehead and held him close. His body was hot to the touch and it jerked from time to time as he lingered between life and death.

The last thing Nathan remembered was seeing the panic in his wife's eyes. The next moment he found himself dreaming—or remembering. He tried to make sense of his surroundings, but he felt disconnected from the events that were unfolding around him. He was standing among a large group of men with swords drawn. Before them on a stone stood an old man leaning on a wooden staff.

Nathan struggled to remember when he had been here; how old this memory was. Then it hit him—it was only the day before that he had stood in this place. He had joined with an Israelite war party that was planning on attacking a small village tucked away in the mountains. The village was not the primary objective, but the gate by which the rest would fall.

He remembered feeling strong and confident. According to the scouting reports, this would be an easy victory. His war party outnumbered the men of the village three to one. The plans were simple: draw the enemy out and then overwhelm them by sure numbers. Nathan remembered drawing out the plans, and then came the voice of the old man, interrupting them. The voice of Moses.

"Do not do this. Do not go up. The Lord is not with you, and you will not succeed." Nathan had responded, "We will not be stopped; we have come too far. We will succeed. We outnumber them, and this will be a great victory for all of us. We can and will take this city, and then you will see how great we are." The old man pleaded with them, but Nathan would not listen. Soon Moses gave up and went back to his tent in sorrow.

In a flash Nathan now found himself in a new surrounding. He was running forward with his sword in his hand. Again he felt somewhat disconnected from the event. Then he remembered that this was exactly what had happened on the battlefield. In memory, he was once again running into battle.

As he ran, his eyes saw light flashing from the right and the left. He soon realized that the enemy was swarming out of the hills and down upon his men from both directions. Screams of horror could be heard on all sides as his friends fell. The heat of the battle rose as the main force from the city pushed through the Israelite front lines. His mind raced as he tried to understand how such a small force could overwhelm them. The battle scene looked like ants attacking an elephant. The size was with Nathan and his men, but the enemy kept coming. Nothing seemed to slow them down.

WHEN WE WILLINGLY CHOOSE TO IGNORE GOD WHEN HE SAYS "NO," IT WILL COME WITH A COST.

"Ahhhhhh!" Nathan screamed as he felt a piercing pain deep within his side. The scream echoed through his memory. Another pain shot up from his left arm and another from his right. His mind said to fight on, but it no longer commanded his body. In anguish and pain he fell to the ground. A horn blew and a shout of retreat could be heard among the ranks. Nathan felt himself being lifted up by many hands and dragged off of the battlefield.

His plans and dreams fell away with each passing moment. What had he been thinking when he so easily disregarded Moses' words? He had followed the man out of slavery and into freedom. It was not what he had thought it would be, but it was more than what he and his family had had before.

An instant later, a light flashed. Nathan longer found himself in the heat of battle—or in the throes of memory. He was kneeling in a throne room, and something told him that he would never see his wife again. He should have heeded Moses. If he had, he would be with his family, instead of facing eternal judgment before God.

The children of Israel tried to go ahead and push their promise through even though God told them, through Moses, that He would not be with them. They would not listen. They chose to ignore the warning and to press forward with their plans. We are no different than the Israelites. When we willingly choose to ignore God when He says "no," it will come with a cost.

None of us enjoy hearing the word "no," however, it is a vital word that most of us learn early on. Growing up, I heard it from my parents a thousand times. I also know that as a kid I would push the limits of my parents' answer. Depending on what I had asked for, I would beg and continue to ask. Sometimes they would give in, but more often than not, they stood by their decision. For the most part, I followed my parents' leading; however, I have to admit that there were times I did not. Many times I found out the hard way that my parents were right. The older I become the more I realize that every time my parents told me no, they did so out of love. Do we respond any differently to God when he says no?

There have been many times I have heard God say no. One particular time stands out above the rest. From a young age I have been in love with politics, and I wanted to live in Washington DC. The chance came up to be the acting manager at a job site there, and I was excited. For sixty days, the company that I was working for put me up in a hotel and I was able to be right in the heart of the place of my dreams. At the end of the sixty days, I was offered the job without even putting in for it. It was amazing—a dream come true!

When I received the job offer, I told the regional manager that I would think about it and get back with her. It had become a habit of mine to always ask advice from men whom I had come to trust before making any large move in life. I also wanted to pray about it to ensure that this move was indeed God's best for me. I was pretty sure God would give me a green light. Why would He say no? This was my dream and it was right in front of me, ready to be fulfilled.

When I prayed and heard the word "no," I could not believe my ears! I asked again and again, but still the word came back: "No, do not take the position." I felt crushed. I wrestled with God about it for another week. I tossed and turned at night, and though everything was going well at work, I could not find peace.

After a week of fighting, I finally submitted to God. When I did, peace passed over me like water. I informed the regional manager that I had decided to turn down the offer and went back to Boston where I was currently stationed. As time went on, things went from bad to worse. One of the Vice Presidents of our company became angry when I did not take the job. From that point on, he tried to find any reason to let me go. I could not understand why God had turned me away from the job of my dreams; still, at every turn God protected me. Then a door opened for me to transfer to a station in Arkansas.

HE SHOWS HIS LOVE FOR US MORE IN THE TIMES WHEN HE SAYS NO THAN WHEN HE SAYS YES.

I turned down the DC job at the Washington Regan Airport in late 2000. The tragic events of September 11, 2001 happened a year later. The airport was shut down for several weeks. Due to cutbacks, the tragic events of 911, and the events that followed, the office went through three managers. Looking back, I could have been one of those managers. Only God could have known ahead of time. I am thankful now that I listened to God. It kept me out of harm's way and protected me from things that I could never have seen coming.

From this experience I learned the valuable lesson of listening to God when He says no. I didn't like it when He turned down my request, but I have come to appreciate His guidance. His love for me, much like that of my parents, has become more apparent to me the more I know Him. I would even dare say that He shows His love for us more in the times when He says no than when He says yes. Just like a parent, He wants us to be happy and blessed, and to enjoy all that He provides. He also knows that, as children, our desires are not always the best things for us. If you have children, would you allow them to eat all of the chocolate they wanted? Most would agree that there is nothing wrong with chocolate, but too much at one time can make you sick. As a parent you know these things, but your child does not.

Some may say that putting things this way is too simple for the real world. Let me assure you that I believe this simple application actually understates the relationship between man and God. He is far greater than we are able to comprehend. He alone created everything, including you and me. Who knows better than He what we should or should not do? He created the universe and knows how it works. He also knows how to bless us and keep us from pain. Consider all of these things the next time God tells you no.

I once heard a saying that I hope you will remember: "A smart man learns from his mistakes, but a smarter man still learns from the mistakes of others." Mistakes happen, but willfully going ahead when God says no is never a smart move to make. The children of Israel learned this lesson the hard way. Will you? When we willfully disobey God, it will cost us. The next time that God says no, how will you respond?

WHEN GOD SAYS "NO"

Numbers 14:41-45

41 And Moses said, "Now why do you transgress the command of the LORD? For this will not succeed. 42 "Do not go up, lest you be defeated by your enemies, for the LORD is not among you. 43 "For the Amalekites and the Canaanites are there before you, and you shall fall by the sword; because you have turned away from the LORD, the LORD will not be with you." 44 But they presumed to go up to the mountaintop; nevertheless, neither the ark of the covenant of the LORD nor Moses departed from the camp. 45 Then the Amalekites and the Canaanites who dwelt in that mountain came down and attacked them, and drove them back as far as Hormah.

Review Questions:

1. Do you have at least one Godly mentor that you can go to for guidance and direction?

____

____

____

____

____

2. Are there times that you find yourself angry with God because He has not yet given you the promise that you have been waiting for?

____

____

____

____

____

3. If God was to tell you to let go of something that appears to be the answer to your prayers, what would your response be?

____

____

____

____

____

Chapter 10

DOUBT IN THE DESERT

And immediately Jesus reached out his hand and caught him and said to him, "O you of little faith,why did you doubt?"
Matthew 14:31

The sun rose above the horizon and Carl knew this was going to be another long and hot day. He could already feel the sand beneath his feet growing warmer with the passing moments. Sweat formed on his brow as the sun's rays cast a shadow on the light brown sand. Shading his eyes with his hand, he looked back on the miles he had covered. His mind retraced each step of the journey.

He remembered the joy and anticipation he had felt on the first day. Everything had been accounted for on his list: water, food, proper clothing, a tent, and most of all a compass. He was sure he had thought of everything. That day now seemed a million miles away, a distant dream more than an actual event in his life. He now realized how foolish he had been—but he could never have imagined how much things would change.

In the deepest part of his heart he knew that this was the way he was supposed to go. His father had chosen this journey for him, and he was bound and determined not to let him down. “Be of good cheer and do not fear, my son. It is vital that you go this way.” His father's words played over and over in his mind. Doubts assailed him, yet he could not doubt his father’s love for him. He chose to put all of his hesitations away and trust in his father’s words.

As the day lengthened, Carl tried with all his heart to believe the words his father had spoken, just as he had tried in the days before, but it was difficult. . A battle raged in his mind, growing fiercer with every step he took. Each time he remembered his father’s words, another thought would follow. “If that was true, then why are you here now with nothing?” His mind focused on the heat of the sun bearing down upon him, the fact that the last drop of water had fallen to his lips hours before, and the hunger that now gripped his body.

Under the weight of his distress he fell to his knees. The pain and disbelief grew deep within until he could no longer contain it. Then, in a moment, it burst forth from his lips in two words: "Father, why?" His soul yearned for a response; his ears waited for the sound of his father's voice. Nothing. No sound could be heard. Another assault was launched against his mind. "Your father does not care about you. You are all alone, and you will die in this desert."

The doubt and pain that consumed his heart was greater than he had ever felt. Desperately he searched his soul for a reason to keep going, and there he found his father's words: "I love you son and I will not leave you." Could his father have known he would come to this very point in his journey? His father had traveled the desert many times and knew all of its ways, so he must have known this time would come.

The words hardly seemed to match the reality that lay before his eyes. Before him Carl saw hills of sand, the unrelenting sun, and a desert that would never end. All of these things told him that there was no hope, yet he could not shake his father's words. Carl knew at that moment that he had to choose: go on or give up. The choice would define the rest of his life.

With every strain of his heart he pushed against the assault of doubt on his mind. He would not surrender to the pain in his body. He refused to give in to the agony of his soul. With great effort, he pulled himself upright and placed one foot in front of the other.

One more step, one more hill, one more day: these were his focus now. He did not think about getting to the other end of the desert. He did not spend time wondering how he would get his next morsel of food or drop of water. His goal was simple—keep moving at all costs.

What Carl did not know was that just over the next hill there was a small village, tucked away in the midst of the desert. His father had known that when his son made it this far he would need new provisions. With this knowledge, Carl's father had gone before him to ensure that all was prepared. He had secured food, water, and shelter for his son. He had even left clothing there for him.

When Carl finally reached the top of the hill, the sight of the village filled him with hope. His spirit jumped within him and he found himself running down the hill with full force. As he reached the center of the village, his body finally gave way and he collapsed.

For a time he was unconscious, and then the sun broke through the tent, its rays bright in Carl's eyes. He sat up and tried to shake the cobwebs from his head. Was he still asleep? Was everything around him just part of a dream? As he rose from the bed, a villager came in and met him. Carl did not say a word as he was led through the village to a large tent. As the flaps of the tent were drawn back, the sunlight fell upon a table that was full of food and drink.

After Carl had had his fill, he was brought new clothes, a map, and even a new compass, all of them familiar to him. All at once he realized where he had seen all these things before. Each item had belonged to his father. In that instant, he knew that his father had known about his struggles before he had taken his first step on this journey. His father knew where the journey would be difficult and how long his provisions would last.

Carl realized that he would have died just a half-mile back if he had stopped moving forward. All of the doubts that had consumed his mind vanished once he saw the provisions his father had prepared for him. All that filled his heart and mind now was the love his father had for him.

The next three days passed quickly as Carl rested in the village. He knew, though, that the time had come for him to finish the journey. He laughed out loud when he recalled that, just a few days before, he had almost completely given up. With a renewed spirit and determination, he began the next leg of his journey. His faith in his father's love was greater than ever before.

THERE WILL BE TIMES WHEN GOD WILL HAVE US GO THROUGH DESERT PERIODS IN OUR LIVES. WE HAVE TO REMEMBER DURING THESE TIMES THAT HE IS NOT PUNISHING US.

A few years ago I found myself surrounded by a different kind of desert. While my spiritual desert was not of sand or sun, it was barren, dry, and very foreign to me. It seemed that everything I had once taken comfort in was now a million miles away.

I grew up in Texas, and by all consideration, I am a southern man. I was taught that a man should hold open doors for ladies as a sign of respect and honor. It was quite normal in my world to say "hello" to strangers in the grocery store and in other public places. Finally, I was taught that the main things of life are God, family, friends, and country.

My mother made sure that God was the center of my life growing up. She was a God-fearing woman, and we were at church every Sunday morning. The truth is that in any town in Texas you will probably see a church on every other corner—if not closer.. So, for most of my life, church was just a part of growing up in the South. Until I moved away from the church I attended, I never realized how much I had taken it for granted.

Another aspect of home I had taken for granted was my family. The saying "Blood is thicker than water" speaks volumes about the way my family interacts with each other. Family is more important than career, objects, or the other attractions of this world. As with most families, my siblings and I fought growing up, but we loved each other and have always stayed close.

When I transferred to Boston, I felt like I was starting my descent into the desert period of my life. The problem was that I did not know the actual extent of the journey I was about to undertake. I was sure I had heard God tell me that this was His plan and that I needed to go. I had even received Godly counsel about the move from pastors that I was close to. But I didn't understand what my decision to go would mean.

I can still remember the morning it dawned on me that I was not only in a new city with a new job, but that I had actually willingly walked into the desert. By taking this step of faith, I had willingly given up everything I had depended upon. The only choice I had now was to fully depend on God.

The sun rose brightly on a Sunday morning early that fall. I was living in a hotel and trying to find an apartment to rent. I had not yet found a church because work had taken up so much of my time.

Since I had not found a local church, my first thought was to find a familiar pastor to watch on the television. In the South, I had become accustomed to being able to turn on the television and select from a dozen pastors to watch. I soon found out that this was not the case in Boston. Church services were not available on the basic cable stations provided by the hotel.

This was a shock to me, however, I decided I would at least tune the radio to a station in order to listen to a church service. I could only find one Christian radio station, and the signal was very faint. I had not planned on this at all and was at a loss as to what to do.

As the days rolled by, I was confronted by the fact that I did not have the equipment or the know-how to survive the coming winter. I had planned for cold, but more for a bad winter in Texas than a normal winter in Boston. As the season came closer, the wind blew harder than I had ever felt before, and it cut through me like a knife. The day that I walked home in a wind chill factor of – 31 degrees will be forever etched in my memory.

My family, friends, and church now lay half a continent away. God had basically stripped everything away from me but Himself. I had no choice but to rely on Him for everything. When I realized this, I knew I had to make a choice. Either I would walk on and have faith in His love for me, or I would run home and quit the journey I had begun. Worry, doubt, and fear attacked my mind. There were many days I did not know how I was going to make it financially or spiritually.

I found myself hanging on to the only thing I had left—faith in God. Through it all, God gave me the faith and strength to continue to walk forward one step at a time. Even though the road was hard, I knew He had caused me to walk this way. I had to finish the journey I had begun, because I knew God had a plan for me even in the desert.

In the coming weeks, God opened my eyes to see Him work in ways I would have never noticed before. First, He provided me with a place to live that I could afford. This was a much-needed miracle due to the fact that I had taken the position for far less than it would actually require to live in Boston.

Next, He guided me in the direction of a church to attend. It would take me 45 min to drive to it on Sunday mornings and over an hour on Wednesday nights due to traffic. I didn't care about the time it took me to drive to the church. I was just thankful I had found a place where I could connect with other Christians. Finally, He provided me with a network of friends who helped me through the many trying times.

The next two years I grew in ways I never thought were possible. Times were hard, and I never really felt at home. However, I realized that God does not call us to the desert so we can feel comfortable. God uses this time to help us grow closer to Him.

WE JUST HAVE TO BE WILLING TO LET GO AND LET GOD DO THE REST. THIS IS THE ONLY WAY TO OVERCOME THE DOUBT THAT WILL COME IN THE DESERT.

There will be times when God will have us go through desert periods in our lives. We have to remember during these times that He is not punishing us. He knows we cannot reach the Promised Land that He has for us unless we are willing to be refined by Him. Refining of gold happens in the heat of the furnace. Our souls, too, are refined in the furnace of life, and sometimes it may seem more than we can bear. While your road may be difficult, let me assure you that God will always provide. We just have to be willing to let go and let God do the rest. This is the only way to overcome the doubt that will come in the desert.

DOUBT IN THE DESERT

Luke 12:27

27 "Consider the lilies, how they grow: they neither toil nor spin; and yet I say to you, even Solomon in all his glory was not arrayed like one of these.

Matthew 6:28

28 "So why do you worry about clothing? Consider the lilies of the field, how they grow: they neither toil nor spin;

Review Questions:

1. Take a few minutes to think about the areas in your life where you might have doubt. What areas do you struggle with concerning doubt?

____
____
____
____
____

2. In your own words, what does Luke 12:27 say? How does that apply to the areas you listed above?

____
____
____
____
____

3. What did David do when he was discouraged in 1 Samuel 30:6? What can we learn from his example?

____
____
____
____
____

Pray

Jesus, help my faith. You know the areas where I doubt, yet I read in Your word that I should not worry. I know I am worth more to You than the flowers of the field and the birds in the air. Please take all of my doubts and worries from me and replace them with faith in Your word.

Now take a moment, close your eyes and ball up your hands. In your hands, visualize the areas where you doubt. Then slowly open your hands and visualize Jesus taking your doubts and worries from you.

Remember, just because you give your doubts to Jesus does not mean they won't try to come back. This is a battle, and if you have to go before Jesus again to give Him your doubts then do so. As your faith grows, be patient with yourself. Growth in all areas of life takes time. If you trust in Jesus and ask Him to help your faith, He will answer you.

Chapter 11
OFF THE BEATEN PATH

For thou art my rock and my fortress;
therefore for thy name's sake lead me, and guide me.
Psalm 31:3

Dawn was breaking on the warm summer day as I pushed back the opening of the tent. I had awakened filled with anticipation. For the last week, I had been part of a group that was backpacking through a mountain range in northern New Mexico. What an adventure it had been! Some may not see a ten-day hike as an adventure, but to this thirteen year old boy that is exactly what it was.

Philmont was the best Boy Scout camp in the nation, and I had been preparing for it for months. It had one focus: experiencing nature as God intended. In the months leading up to that summer, my fellow Scouts and I carried backpacks filled with gear around a local lake. Even though I had always been very active, I knew I was nowhere near ready for Philmont. Week after week we would hike around the lake, preparing for the summer.

The weeks soon turned into months. Each time we went out, the journey became less of a hardship. Soon the day came for us to make the long drive from Dallas, Texas to northern New Mexico. I remember very little about the actual drive, except for the fact that we could not get there fast enough. We were all filled with excitement, which made sleep along the way very difficult.

Once we reached Philmont, we set up camp and tried to get some much needed rest. I remember thinking that this would be the last day for a while that I would be sleeping on anything remotely similar to a bed. For the next ten days the earth would be my mattress—and no matter how many pine needles I put under my tent, it still was not like home.

The night passed quickly, and I soon found myself standing in front of a cabin receiving the dehydrated food that would last me for the next three or four days. Once my pack was laden down with everything I could carry, I was ready to hit the trail. A full pack, weighing forty or fifty pounds, may not feel like a lot—but once you've carried it for ten days, it feels like a boulder tied to your back.

I fell into line behind another Scout, and off we went into the deep woods that lay ahead. "Be Prepared" was the Scout motto, and we were. We had maps, a compass, water, food, and enough energy to take on the world. With only a quick glance back, we said good-bye to civilization and embraced the wilderness before us.

As the first day of our journey came to a close, we had covered close to seven miles. The path that day was well-traveled, a level trail with few inclines. Even so, when my head hit my pillow that evening and my body rested on the ground, I felt as though I was in the best hotel in Dallas. Sleep quickly overtook me, and the hours between night and day seemed to pass as only seconds.

The next few days the path became more difficult and our trips a bit longer. By the end of each day I could feel in my bones that we had traveled a great way, but when morning came I was ready to go again. Each day was different, and the beauty I beheld in those days will be forever held in my memory.

It was important for us to know that we were not just wandering aimlessly in the wilderness. In fact, we had a very exact destination, and though none of us had seen it, we knew it existed. We had been told about it, we had seen pictures of it, and the map we followed told us where it was located. Our destination was Mt. Baldy, the highest peak in the camp.

Before we would reach this point, we would climb many miles and have more adventures than I can recount. One adventure that stands out in my memory is that of a time when we were heading down a path that was supposed to take us to our next supply stop. We had been hiking for most of the morning, and the sun was high in the sky above. While hot rays of sunlight fell through the thick pines, the cool breeze of the mountain could still be felt.

One of the older Scouts had taken the lead and was using a compass and the map to navigate our way though the almost impregnable forest. All of us knew that the supply station lay in a valley between this mountain and the next; however, none of us could remember any of the trails being this thick before. As we marched on, we could see a break in the trees in front of us. We soon realized we had made it to the far side of the mountain. We stood on a ledge that overlooked a valley vibrant with beauty.

"There," someone called out as he pointed to the cabin tucked away among the trees. Yes, finally we could see our destination. We were flooded with relief. Just a few hours earlier some of us (including myself) had wondered if we would make it to our next stop before sunset. We were running low on supplies and it was imperative that we restock in the next day or so.

Our elation soon gave way to overwhelming alarm. Where had the path gone? None of us could see a path from the point where we were standing to the supply station below. We all spread out and looked, but no path could be found.

Then one of the Scouts pointed to the path that we needed to take. There was only one problem: it was halfway down the mountain. At that moment, we realized that at some point early in the morning we had gotten off of the right path. We had two choices. We could backtrack to the path (though no one could remember where we had gotten off course or even if we could go back the exact way we had come), or we could make our own path down the side of the mountain to the supply stop we saw in the distance.

We debated both positions, but it was obvious to everyone that we needed supplies. If we turned around, we might never find the path. So off we went, down the side of the mountain. A close friend and I led this time, and we picked the best path possible. It was not an easy descent, but it had to be made. We projected that it would take us about two hours to climb down the mountain. We realized our estimations were wrong when the sun began to set in the west. Knowing we had to make it down before the sun disappeared behind the distant mountain, we pressed on.

We finally reached the dirt road as the sun fell behind the mountain peak. I remember having to force my body to move the last hundred yards to the cabin. Exhausted by the journey, we all ate dinner quietly and then turned in for the night. At that moment, we did not care how we had gotten off track. We were simply thankful to the Lord above for somehow getting us to our destination.

The next morning we studied the map and realized where we had made our mistake. If we had chosen to backtrack the night before, it would have taken us four hours to get back to the path and then another four to six hours to make it to the cabin.

While backtracking would have lost us time, the reality is that if we had stayed on the right path in the first place we would have arrived at our destination hours before we actually did. We would also have been able to bypass the trees, brush, and steep inclines that we had to go through to get back on the right road.

BY CHOOSING OUR OWN PATH TO THE DREAM THAT GOD HAS GIVEN US, WE ARE SAYING THAT WE KNOW BETTER THAN GOD.

Many times in life it seems that we find ourselves searching for the right path to take. There are times we choose to follow our own way to the destination instead of waiting for God to show us His way. It may seem that we know what needs to be done and so we go ahead, not paying attention to the markers that show us the right way to go. By choosing our own path to the dream that God has given us, we are saying that we know better than God. While most of us would never tell God with our words that we know best, we often do so with our actions.

So what do we do when we find ourselves off of the path that God has planned for us? Let us look and see what someone close to God's heart did. Maybe his example can help us gleam some wisdom on how to best handle the situation when it arises in our own lives.

The night was balmy and warm. The heat of the summer had come early this year. The king sat in his war room, looking at the plans that he and his generals had drawn up over the last few months. As he sat going over the battle plan in detail, he was filled with both anticipation and nervousness.

For just a moment he sat back in his chair and closed his eyes. As he did so he could see the battle as it converged. He had known war since the day of his youth. He could sense the flow of the conflict, even feel the heat of battle as it waged on. The sounds of war rushed into his ears, and visions of fallen warriors filled his mind.

He could remember his brothers going out to war when he was still very young. He himself had spent his first summer of war as a teenager. How many thousands of men had lived their final moments in his grasp? How many of his fallen comrades had he prayed for as their final breath left them? He had lost count long ago, but each one lay heavy upon his heart. He had always known that being a strong leader meant making hard decisions, but now he longed for rest.

In the last several weeks as the weather had started turning warmer, he had begun to fight an inward battle. He knew he ought to go to war with his men, but he was tired of war, and there were thousands of young men who would fight for him. Therefore, just a week before, he had decided that this year he was going to stay in the capital city and enjoy the success God had given him.

As he sat with his head in his hand, his mind consumed with thoughts of the war he was trying to escape, a hand gently touched his shoulder. He reacted as if he were being attacked. In a matter of seconds he had the man pinned against the wall, his strong fingers around the servant's throat. "My king, my king!" the servant screamed in shock. The familiar voice awakened him to his senses.

As quickly as he had grabbed his servant, the king released him. He was spending too much time worrying about the impending war—it was the only way to explain his reaction. This summer was to be his time of rest, and he was determined to find a way to make use of it.

"Leave me," the king told his servant with a wave of his hand. He quickly turned and headed toward his private sanctuary. There was only one place in the entire palace that he could truly find peace, high above the chaos that now surrounded him: on the palace roof. The palace was the highest building in the entire city, and from its roof the king could see for miles.

The king loved to watch from the roof as the city pulsated with life below him. On this particular night the moon hung high in the night sky, and its fullness seemed to overpower the few stars that danced around it. A mild cool breeze was blowing out of the west and the king could smell the salt of the sea.

The moon cast a veil of light upon the city, drawing back the darkness that tried in vain to conceal the beauty now visible to the king's eyes. The king felt his pulse begin to race as his breath came more rapidly. With an outstretched hand he pointed to a rooftop in the distance. The king then ordered one of his servants to find out the identity of the woman who was bathing there.

Soon his servant returned, telling the king that the woman he was watching was the wife of one of his most trusted warriors. This information did not deter the king. He allowed his eyes to linger. He had already decided in his heart that he would have this woman as his own. Without a moment of hesitation, he instructed his servant to bring her to the palace.

As the hours passed, the king's anticipation grew, and so did the lust within his heart. Just at the moment he thought he could wait no longer, the doors of his chamber flew open. There before him stood the beautiful woman he had seen from the palace roof a short time before. He quickly dismissed all of his servants, leaving them alone together. The woman now knew why she had been summoned—and she knew that she could not deny the king.

As soon as the king had yielded to the lust of his flesh and spent the evening with the woman, he knew that he was guilty of sin. The morning would soon arrive, and he secretly arranged for the woman to leave the palace. Under the cover of darkness, just before dawn the woman was ushered to her home. The king thought he had achieved his goal. After all, he had not been caught.

Weeks had passed since the time of their first encounter. The king desperately wanted to see the woman, but he could not take the chance of being caught. It was only by luck and timing that he had gotten away with the last visit. Only the servants knew—and they would not dare cross the king.

As he sat upon his throne, thinking of how he could arrange to see her again, a servant came in with a message for the king's eyes only. At first he thought the message was from the front line. He had not heard a word from his commander in days, and he was eagerly waiting for updates about the battle. These thoughts retreated into a distant part of his mind as he unfolded the paper that now lay in his hand.

The letter was not from the commander. No, this was a letter from the woman that now held his heart. As he read each word carefully, he felt as if he were looking down upon himself from another location. The note was simple and to the point: "I am with child."

WE ALL FALL SHORT, AND SOMETIMES WE WILL WALK OFF THE PATH—EITHER INTENTIONALLY OR UNINTENTIONALLY. HOWEVER, WE MUST ALL BE WILLING TO BE GUIDED BACK TO IT.

Stunned, he took a breath as the life drained from his face. "Can this be true?" he asked himself. He closed his eyes and saw his kingdom fall apart before him. No, there had to be a way to make sure this secret would stay hidden for all time. It was too late to undo what he had done. He had already committed to this path, and so he began to chart out his next moves. He began to plot a way through the moral minefield where he now found himself.

This man is known today as one of the greatest kings to rule over Israel. His feats and victories are still spoken about thousands of years later, but we also remember the moment when everything could have been lost. After King David spent the night with Bathsheba, she conceived a child. To cover this up, David tried to convince her husband to return from battle and sleep with her. Her husband Uriah did return, but out of honor and respect for the men he fought beside, he refused to go into his house. Instead, he spent his nights on the ground at the palace gate. King David failed to get Uriah to go to his wife, so the king sent him back to the front lines with a message to the general of the armies of Israel. In that message was a plan that would directly lead to the death of Uriah, clearing the way for David to take Bathsheba to be his wife.

WHEN WE CHOOSE TO GO AGAINST HIS DIRECTION WE MUST UNDERSTAND THAT THERE WILL BE A PRICE TO PAY.

King David chose to step off the path God had placed him on; just as my friends and I chose to step off the path in the woods while backpacking in New Mexico. Our mistake took us deep into the woods and down a mountain pass that was both difficult and dangerous. One of our Scout leaders was injured on the descent, and we almost did not make it to our destination before nightfall. King David's choice cost him much more. The affair that he thought he had covered up was soon exposed to the world. The son that was conceived in the sinful act became deathly ill and soon died. Finally, those around him paid the price of his misstep. War, incest, rebellion, and infighting followed his family for many generations: all of this because he chose to step off the path God had for him and he yielded to his flesh.

When King David was approached about the matter by the prophet Nathan, he admitted his sin and fell broken before the Lord. For this reason God forgave him. God picked him up from the crooked path he found himself on and placed him back on the right path. This willingness to be broken and forgiven is something we must all embrace.

We all fall short, and sometimes we will walk off the path—either intentionally or unintentionally. However, we must all be willing to be guided back to it. If we truly desire to reach the destination God has for us, then we must follow His directions. We have the right to choose, but when we choose to go against His direction we must understand that there will be a price to pay. The good news is that when we are lost in the woods of our lives we can take heart in knowing that we serve a God who will show us the right way if only we will ask. Ask yourself: are you off the beaten path? Are you willing do whatever it takes to get back on the path that God has for you? He is waiting for you. What will you choose this day?

OFF THE BEATEN PATH

2 Samuel 11:1-15

1 It happened in the spring of the year, at the time when kings go out to battle, that David sent Joab and his servants with him, and all Israel; and they destroyed the people of Ammon and besieged Rabbah. But David remained at Jerusalem. 2 Then it happened one evening that David arose from his bed and walked on the roof of the king's house. And from the roof he saw a woman bathing, and the woman was very beautiful to behold. 3 So David sent and inquired about the woman. And someone said, "Is this not Bathsheba, the daughter of Eliam, the wife of Uriah the Hittite?" 4 Then David sent messengers, and took her; and she came to him, and he lay with her, for she was cleansed from her impurity; and she returned to her house. 5 And the woman conceived; so she sent and told David, and said, "I am with child." 6 Then David sent to Joab, saying, "Send me Uriah the Hittite." And Joab sent Uriah to David. 7 When Uriah had come to him, David asked how Joab was doing, and how the people were doing, and how the war prospered. 8 And David said to Uriah, "Go down to your house and wash your feet." So Uriah departed from the king's house, and a gift of food from the king followed him. 9 But Uriah slept at the door of the king's house with all the servants of his lord, and did not go down to his house. 10 So when they told David, saying, "Uriah did not go down to his house," David said to Uriah, "Did you not come from a journey? Why did you not go down to your house?" 11 And Uriah said to David, "The ark and Israel and Judah are dwelling in tents, and my lord Joab and the servants of my lord are encamped in the open fields. Shall I then go to my house to eat and drink, and to lie with my wife? As you live, and as your soul lives, I will not do this thing." 12 Then David said to Uriah, "Wait here today also, and tomorrow I will let you depart." So Uriah remained in Jerusalem that day and the next. 13 Now when David called him, he ate and drank before him; and he made him drunk. And at evening he went out to lie on his bed with the servants of his lord, but he did not go down to his house. 14 In the morning it happened that David wrote a letter to Joab and sent it by the hand of Uriah. 15 And he wrote in the letter, saying, "Set Uriah in the forefront of the hottest battle, and retreat from him, that he may be struck down and die."

2 Samuel 11:26-27

26 When the wife of Uriah heard that Uriah her husband was dead, she mourned for her husband. 27 And when her mourning was over, David sent and brought her to his house, and she became his wife and bore him a son. But the thing that David had done displeased the LORD.

2 Samuel 12:10-14

10 'Now therefore, the sword shall never depart from your house, because you have despised Me, and have taken the wife of Uriah the Hittite to be your wife.' 11 "Thus says the LORD: 'Behold, I will raise up adversity against you from your own house; and I will take your wives before your eyes and give them to your neighbor, and he shall lie with your wives in the sight of this sun. 12 'For you did it secretly, but I will do this thing before all Israel, before the sun.' " 13 So David said to Nathan, "I have sinned against the LORD." And Nathan said to David, "The LORD also has put away your sin; you shall not die. 14 "However, because by this deed you have given great occasion to the enemies of the LORD to blaspheme, the child also who is born to you shall surely die."

Review Questions:

1. Have you ever found your self off the beaten path? If so, take a moment and reflect on that time.

____

____

____

____

____

2. What are some choices that you made that got you to that point?

____

____

____

____

____

3. What were some of the warning signs that you were heading down the wrong path?

____

____

____

____

4. Take a moment and reflect on what you have shared. What are some practical steps that you can take to ensure that you do not go off the beaten path again?

____
____
____
____
____

5. Are there any actions or habits that you have condoned in your life that God is telling you to give up?

____
____
____
____
____

Pray:

Lord, You alone know what lies around the next corner. You know the direction You have for me and You know the destination. Please keep me on Your path and open my mind, heart, and spirit to any and all warning signs when I begin to stray. Do not let my heart be hardened or closed to Your word and guidance. In Jesus' name, amen.

Chapter 12

SAILING ON WITHOUT THE WIND

And let us not grow weary while doing good,
for in due season we shall reap if we do not lose heart.
Galatians 6:9

Up and down the swells rolled upon the sea. The boat was carried high and then disappeared as it sank with the waves, only to be brought up again. For days now the boat had floated along, but the sailors could not tell if progress was being made.

They had begun their journey months ago and had bonded through their experiences. They had endured storms that could have swamped the boat. The hot sun had darkened their skin, and the long lonely nights upon the sea had laid siege to their hearts. They had fought it all: wind, rain, sun, disease, fear; and through it all, they had grown stronger.

For some of the sailors the voyage was proving harder than they had expected. Promises of great bounty, freedom, and far-off destinations had lured them in. The older sailors had seen this before. They knew that not everyone would still be with them when they reached their final destination. They knew that some were just not cut out for this kind of life.

Six months at sea, away from family and the comforts of home, could wear on a man. Yet the older sailors knew that the riches that awaited them were greater than the struggles they had to live through. They had all lived through the doubts, worries, and fears of the sea. For them, the voice of experience drowned out the clamor of fear. They recalled the promises of the Captain, and with each successful voyage their faith in him grew.

Faith in the word of the Captain was the one thing that kept the old sailors on task no matter the obstacles. The younger sailors struggled with faith in the promise of rewards not yet seen. The sea strained their faith and the waves tossed doubt into their minds.

Even now, on a calm, warm day, they wondered if indeed their Captain knew the way.

What had brought on the doubts and fears? There was no storm to blame, food was in plenty, and the waters were still. The answer could be found in the main mast of the ship. From the center mast hung a large sail that, when filled with air, would push the ship along the deep blue waters. When the wind blew the large sail would be stretched out and like a large hand would catch the wind. When the wind changed direction, orders would be given and the sail would be moved to capture the wind once again.

The young sailors had begun to put their trust in it. Even in the hard times of the voyage, they would remind each other that as long as the wind blew, they knew they would make it to their destination. As the days and weeks went on they depended more on the sail and less on the words of the Captain. Before their eyes they could see the power of the wind and the purpose of the sail, while their hearts failed to be captured by the promises of the Captain.

So it was with great disbelief and heartache that the younger sailors met the day that the wind stopped blowing. As they stood staring at the now-limp sail, their hearts fell like the waves upon the sea. The Captain called out to them to reassure them, but his words fell on deaf ears. The older sailors tried to tell them that the wind would return. At first this lifted their spirits, but with each passing hour they believed less and less.

The Captain and the older sailors had seen this before. They had lived on the sea a long time, and they knew the wind would eventually return. Until it did, they would continue repairing the ship. They did not allow their spirits to fall, but instead chose to believe that the best was yet to come.

Days passed, and with each sunrise the Captain and older sailors became more and more excited. Their faith was strong. Deep within their hearts, they knew the wind would return. They also knew that with each passing sunset they were closer to the final destination. The younger sailors could not understand—they failed to see any improvement in their situation. The sail still hung limp. The only movement was the rising and falling of the waves.

IF YOU WERE ON THIS BOAT WHICH SAILOR WOULD YOU BE?

I remember a day when I must admit I would have fallen in with the young, inexperienced sailors. The day had started out promisingly. I had set a goal at work and everything was moving toward it. The waters were a little choppy, but there wasn't much to be concerned about. Then, in a matter of hours, the wind that had been pushing me onward failed.

I was short-staffed. We had worked short for weeks, and my staff was weary. Even so, we had a game plan together to hold things together for another week or so, and then we trusted that things would improve. We had new people in training, and a new schedule was coming out. Things were heading in the right direction. We looked forward to finally being at full strength.

Yet our hope soon turned to despair. First, I had a short encounter with one of my employees in which he told me that he was leaving the company immediately, without proper notice. Next, I was informed that one of my new employees in training was ill and had been rushed to the hospital. Finally, I received a call stating that a third employee would be out for another month.

I felt like I had the wind knocked out of me. My mind raced as I tried to cover the shortages. We had all been riding high on the idea that soon the workload would ease. Now it seemed that I would have to go to my employees once more and tell them that it would not. I could feel my hope and faith fail as I asked the question, "God—how much longer?"

I struggled with what to do and how to do it, only to come to the realization that there was nothing that I could do. All the steps I could take to solve the problem had already been taken. Now it was up to God. Over the next several hours I struggled with the situation. I had trusted more in what I had seen in my hands than in God's ability. While in my head I knew that He alone could meet my needs, I allowed doubt in my heart.

In the calms of life, God wants us to look to Him and trust His words. If He says that He will move the mountain, then the mountain will be moved. If He says that the wind will blow again, then it will blow. If He gives you a promise, it will come to pass.

THOUGH THE HANDS OF GOD IN YOUR LIFE ARE MOVING, YOU MAY NOT SEE THEM.

God's ability to fulfill the promises in our lives does not depend upon our review of His progress. He is not bound by what is seen. When He works, the groundwork is often done without any of us knowing. Who can see the changing of one's heart?

We will all experience times when we feel as if the wind has been knocked out of our sails. We will have times of despair and loneliness along this journey to our promise. If you are experiencing this time right now, or have done so, guess what? You're normal, and God still loves you.

Though the hands of God in your life are moving, you may not see them. You may not feel His presence in your circumstances, and you may even question where He is. All of these feelings are normal. However, all of them must be pushed aside by faith. It is vital that we grow in our walk with Christ to the point that we believe more in the word of God than in the things before our eyes. The world says seeing is believing, but God says believing must come before we will ever see our promises fulfilled.

Go forth today with joy and remember the faith of the saints before you—the older sailors. Every hour the wind fails to blow is another hour closer to its return. Even when you do not see progress in your journey, God is preparing the way. Remember God this day, for He has not forgotten about you.

SAILING ON WITHOUT THE WIND

Galatians 6:7-9

7 Do not be deceived, God is not mocked; for whatever a man sows, that he will also reap. 8 For he who sows to his flesh will of the flesh reap corruption, but he who sows to the Spirit will of the Spirit reap everlasting life. 9 And let us not grow weary while doing good, for in due season we shall reap if we do not lose heart.

Review Questions:

1. How long have you been waiting to see your promise fulfilled?

___
___
___
___

2. Are you willing to endure the journey from where you are today to where your promise lies?

___
___
___
___

3. What steps are you taking today to prepare your life for the promise that God has for you?

___
___
___
___

Chapter 13
WHEN IT'S TIME TO CROSS OVER, YOU WON'T HAVE TO SWIM

39 Then Pharaoh said to Joseph, "Inasmuch as God has shown you all this, there is no one as discerning and wise as you. 40 You shall be over my house, and all my people shall be ruled according to your word; only in regard to the throne will I be greater than you."
Gen 41:39-40

"Mommy, look!" the young boy called out. Aviva's youngest child tugged on her clothing as he cried for her attention. With one arm, the boy clung to his mother's side as he pointed with the other. His mother could remember doing the same thing to her parents as they crossed the Red Sea. She had been a small child then, but there are some memories that stay with you for a lifetime.

Aviva found herself caught up in the miracle that now surrounded her. Just days before her family had been camping near the Jordan River. They had planned to cross it once the rushing waters had receded. This time of year always brought floodwaters down from the mountain, so, though she chafed at the wait, Aviva told herself that there was nothing that could be done about it.

As she began preparing the evening meal, Aviva had accepted the fact that they would be staying put for a while. That was why it caught her by surprise when her husband came bursting in the tent door. Breathless, he told her to start packing. "Three days is all we have until we cross the river," he kept saying. Aviva had gently laid her hand on his shoulder, hoping to calm him long enough to find out was going on. It was then that her husband relayed to her what their new leader, Joshua, had told the people. The leader's instructions were simple: prepare to cross the river in three days.

Aviva hadn't been able to make any sense of it. As she packed the donkey, she had taken a moment to look around. In every direction, as far as her eyes could see, everyone was looking toward the eastern bank of the

Jordan River. Near its banks, the priests stood holding a golden chest. This was no ordinary chest. It was the Ark of the Covenant, and it represented God Himself.

Everyone, including Aviva, knew that if the Ark went before them it was a sign that God was going before them. When God went before them, miracles happened. Aviva knew in her spirit that this time would be no different. As she pondered these things, the silence of the morning was shattered by the sound of the camp's horns. The priests moved toward the Jordan River, carrying the Ark of the Covenant.

The water of the river slowly flowed over the feet of the priests. Once the Ark was fully over the flooding Jordan, they stood still. In an instant, the water at their feet began to rush away. In a matter of minutes, the river waters went racing in opposite directions from each other.

Aviva could hardly believe her eyes. She had seen this happen only once before, and that day was now just a distant memory. She had been a child when the waters of the Red Sea had drawn back. She remembered being picked up in her father's arms as they crossed. Then, they had been running from an army that was set on destroying them. This time, however, as they moved toward the dry river bed, the people took their time crossing.

Together, Aviva and her family began to cross the Jordan. Aviva tried to keep her eyes on her children, but she had been taken back by the experience. She felt the warmth of God around her. She felt the dry pebbles below her feet, and a joy in her spirit that she could not describe. Somehow, deep within, she knew that this was the beginning of their dreams coming true. She was crossing over to the Promised Land on dry ground.

THE CROSSING OF THE JORDAN RIVER REPRESENTED MORE THAN JUST ONE MORE OBSTACLE TO OVERCOME. IT WAS THE LAST HURDLE BETWEEN A PROMISE GIVEN AND A PROMISE FULFILLED.

For forty years the children of Israel had journeyed to the Promised Land. God had taken them from captivity into a land of hardship. He had guided them from a land of plenty to a desert of destitution. He had met with them at the foot of a mountain and guided them through the desert sands. Through every war, challenge, and obstacle, their faith in Him had grown. They went from being a people that depended on themselves to being a people that would not go forward unless He led them.

The crossing of the Jordan River represented more than just one more obstacle to overcome. It was the last hurdle between a promise given and a promise fulfilled. It was the doorway to the land of milk and honey.

The journey you must take may be long and hard, but be of good cheer! It will end. When God's timing is right, all the pieces will fall into place as if they had always been there. I know that for some this is hard to image, but I have seen it time and time again.

Recently I was speaking to a friend whom I had not seen in years. I called him so we could catch up, and I told him I thought I might fly out to see him. He told me that he would love to see me, but that he was getting married in less than a week. He and his new bride would then be heading out of the country for two weeks on their honeymoon.

I was taken aback by the news, but was very excited to hear that my friend had found someone to spend his life with. The last time we had spoken, neither of us was in a relationship. We were both waiting for God to guide us to the right person; and taking it one day at a time.

I asked him how it felt to finally be getting married after waiting so long. He said, "You know, all the years I have waited for my wife seemed to have been washed away. All the longing, loneliness, and doubt have just disappeared." He went on to tell me how happy he was. As he spoke, all I wanted to do was celebrate with him. God had fulfilled a promise in his life, and the joy he now felt more than made up for all of the years of waiting.

WHEN GOD'S TIMING IS RIGHT, ALL THE PIECES WILL FALL INTO PLACE AS IF THEY HAD ALWAYS BEEN THERE.

There have been a number of occasions in the lives of those around me when I have seen God answer prayers overnight. Some needed healing;

others were waiting for loved ones to be saved; others for jobs. Each of them had to experience waiting before they could experience the joy of the promise. Just as He did for the Israelites, God guided them through with hope and faith. In every circumstance they had to walk in faith. When God told them to step out they did so, even though they did not see how their promise would come to pass.

Instead of trusting in themselves or in what lay before them, they chose to trust in God. The journey sometimes seemed unbearable, but, like my friend with his new wife, each said that when the promise was received it washed all of the pain of the past away. When we receive the fulfillment of a promise from God, we too will feel the same.

WHEN IT'S TIME TO CROSS OVER, YOU WON'T HAVE TO SWIM

Joshua 3:13-17

13 "And it shall come to pass, as soon as the soles of the feet of the priests who bear the ark of the LORD, the Lord of all the earth, shall rest in the waters of the Jordan, that the waters of the Jordan shall be cut off, the waters that come down from upstream, and they shall stand as a heap." 14
So it was, when the people set out from their camp to cross over the Jordan, with the priests bearing the ark of the covenant before the people, 15 and
as those who bore the ark came to the Jordan, and the feet of the priests who bore the ark dipped in the edge of the water (for the Jordan overflows all its banks during the whole time of harvest), 16 that the waters which
came down from upstream stood still, and rose in a heap very far away at Adam, the city that is beside Zaretan. So the waters that went down into the Sea of the Arabah, the Salt Sea, failed, and were cut off; and the people crossed over opposite Jericho. 17 Then the priests who bore the ark of the
covenant of the LORD stood firm on dry ground in the midst of the Jordan; and all Israel crossed over on dry ground, until all the people had crossed completely over the Jordan.

Review Questions:

1. Is there an area in your life that you need to prepare before crossing over to the promise God has for you?

____

____

____

____

2. List any fears that seem to be keeping you from your promise.

____

____

____

____

3. What went before the Israelites as they crossed the Jordan River?

4. What did it represent?

5. Are you allowing things in the natural to keep you from receiving the supernatural promise that God has given you?

6. Are you willing to trust in God each step of the way?

Chapter 14

ENDURING THE STORMS OF LIFE

23 The steps of a good man are ordered by the Lord,
And He delights in his way. 24 Though he fall,
he shall not be utterly cast down;
For the Lord upholds him with His hand.
Psalms 37:23-24

The solider stoked the fire as he tried to distract himself from the upcoming battle. Embers rose into the night and disappeared as quickly as they had risen. The crackle of the fire was the only sound that could be heard. Each man's eyes stared into the flames that danced in the dark, every mind captured with thoughts of what lay ahead.

Most of the fighting men in the camp were young. The enemy they now faced was mighty, and not like any they had fought against before. Tension lingered in the air, and it laid heavily on each man's spirit. Finally, the silence was broken as the youngest man spoke. "Sir, are you sure we will win this battle?"

For a moment no response came, and then the oldest man in the group raised his head and looked directly into the young soldier's eyes. The young solider could see the reflection of the fire in his leader's eyes—to him, they seemed to be coming from deep within the man.

Joshua knew that the young solider was looking for reassurance, and he had no intention of leaving any doubt in the young man's mind. He cleared his throat, raised his head, and ensured that he spoke loudly enough for everyone around the fire to hear.

"Son, you were too young to remember, but long ago I stood next to your father as we fought our first battle. It was in the early years of this campaign, and none of us had been on the battlefield before. We were all nervous, but we were also filled with anticipation, much like each of you today.

"Heat from the sun fell upon us and our skin felt like it was on fire. The sun hung high in the sky and no clouds could be seen. As I stood near the edge of the cliff overlooking the valley below, all I could see was the enemy. Like thousands of ants, they filled the valley floor. Their numbers overwhelmed me, and I felt the last bit of confidence drain from my soul.

At that moment I felt a hand on my shoulder and heard a voice call out to me. I turned and saw that the man who stood next to me was none other than the great leader of our people, Moses himself.

"Even now, thinking back on that moment, I don't know why he singled me out, but he gave me a charge that I had to fulfill. He ordered me to choose some good men and go down and fight the enemy below. The enemy we faced that day was both skilled and battle tested. They were mercenaries that had been raised in the art of war.

"I went throughout the camp choosing the mightiest men I could find. Together we marched to meet the enemy. We went into battle knowing we did not go alone. Moses had promised us that God would go before us and that victory was assured. Our eyes only saw what was before us; however we chose to believe in the God that had delivered us from slavery.

"The day was long, and many men lost their lives. However, as the sun set on the horizon, victory was assured. Against overwhelming odds, God had brought us through the battle. Because He did this, our faith in Him was strengthened. Between that day and this we have gone through many battles. During each one we have learned many things, but the most important thing was that, with each victory, our faith in God continued to grow.

"Do not let your faith fail you now, as we sit here within the shadows of this city. The walls of stone may bring security to those within them. However, we know that our security is found in the arms of our God. He has not led us this far for us to fail. He has not brought us through the storms of battle to see us fall even as we enter into the promise He has given us. He has always been faithful along the way, guiding us, delivering us, and leading us to this very moment.

"Remember the past and the victories He has given us. Recall the path He has used to bring us to this point. Finally, remember the promises He has given us. He alone is able to deliver this city and this land into our hands. He alone will bring all of His promises to pass. He only asks us to have faith and to be obedient to the call. Do not give up now!!! "

Joshua's words reached into the souls of the men around him. Their faith, weighed down only moments before, now burned out of control. As Joshua's last words fell from his lips, the men were on their feet. The passion that had arisen from the leader now set off an explosion of praise and worship throughout the camp.

The noise of the camp rose high above, reaching the walls that surrounded the mighty city. In the watchtowers high above, soldiers stood listening to the noise below. Just moments before they had boasted in pride about the strength of their city, but now they began shaking in fear. Somehow, deep within them, they knew that the battle had already been lost.

As I write this chapter, I can hear the thunder as it rumbles outside. Just a few hours ago it was bright and sunny. The summer has been hot and dry, but for the past week or so thunderstorms have popped up in the afternoon.

JUST LIKE THEIR FAITH, OUR FAITH HAS TO GROW BEFORE WE CAN RECEIVE OUR PROMISE.

Growing up in Dallas, I could see the summer storms coming from miles away. They would move steadily east, and I could prepare for them as they came. For the most part in the summer I looked forward to them, because I knew they would leave as quickly as they came. When we go through storms in our lives, we would like them to come and go in the same way.

Unfortunately, the storms of life are sometimes like the rain I experienced while living in Boston. These storms would move in from the west, but once they were over the city they would stall. For days it would rain without ceasing. Seldom did these storms bring the lightning or deafening thunder of Texas storms; however, they were persistent and seemed to last forever.

As we continue on the journey from the promise given to the promise fulfilled, we too will go through storms. Some of the storms will come up out of nowhere, while others will seem to drag on and on. These storms can involve family, work, or many areas of life.

I have recently gone through a period of about three weeks where it seemed that everything that could go wrong did. At work it seemed that every day I would receive another bit of bad news. Every time I thought I'd hit bottom, the floor would open up and I would fall again.

Searching for answers, I looked for some reason why things were going badly. Was there something I had done, or something I had failed to do? I prayed, read, and prayed some more. I asked for advice and listened to sermons, and the only answer I heard was one word: "endurance."

Two million Israelites began a forty-year journey with just one step. They finished it because they endured through the storms of life. If at any point along the way they had chosen to turn back, they would never have received their promise.

YOU CAN MAKE IT THROUGH THE STORMS IF YOU CHOOSE TO ENDURE.

Our Christian life and journey to God's promise is exactly the same way. We must endure the storms of life so that we too may lay hold of the promises that God has given us. Each day as we rise, we have a choice to endure or to give in.

The recent storm that I went through finally came to an end, and I now find myself on the other side. I can tell you with confidence that the rewards are worth every day I had to endure. Let me share with you a saying that helps me endure during the trials of life:

"Today as I awake, I am one day closer to the promise that God has given me and another day closer to the journey's end."

Have you ever gone through a storm in life? Did it trouble you that you could not see the reason God allowed these things to happen?

Trust me: you can make it through the storms if you choose to endure. If the Israelites had not gone through war, they would never have laid hold of the Promised Land. If their faith had not been challenged, it would have never grown.

It will take faith to receive the promise that God has given you. When the children of Israel started their journey, they did not have faith large enough to receive their promise. Just like their faith, our faith has to grow before we can receive our promise. Do you have the faith today to receive your promise from God? Are you willing to endure life's storms to receive your promise?

ENDURING THE STORMS OF LIFE

Joshua 4:15-19

15 Then the LORD spoke to Joshua, saying, 16 "Command the priests who bear the ark of the Testimony to come up from the Jordan." 17 Joshua therefore commanded the priests, saying, "Come up from the Jordan." 18 And it came to pass, when the priests who bore the ark of the covenant of the LORD had come from the midst of the Jordan, and the soles of the priests' feet touched the dry land, that the waters of the Jordan returned to their place and overflowed all its banks as before. 19 Now the people came up from the Jordan on the tenth day of the first month, and they camped in Gilgal on the east border of Jericho.

Review Questions:

1. Why did God not allow the children of Israel to camp at the southern part of the Promised Land until the forty years had past?

____

____

____

____

2. Why did God lead the Israelites through the trials and tribulations they had to endure in the desert?

____

____

____

____

3. Would the Israelites have been able to possess the Promised Land if they had not been brought through the storms of life?

____

____

____

____

4. Where are you along this journey to the promise that God has given you?

5. Are you at the point where Joshua was when he was first given charge of the men of Israel to fight the Amalekites?

6. Are you in the desert knowing that you are on the way to your promise, but not knowing when it will come?

7. Or maybe you are sitting on the banks of your Jordan within eyesight of your promise, but not knowing how to get there?

8. Why has God brought you the way that He has?

9. Is there something that God wants you to learn in the storms of life so that you can possess the promise He has for you?

Chapter 15

BEYOND THE WALLS OF JERICHO

Where there is no vision, the people perish:
Proverbs 29:18 (KJV)

Joshua knelt just inside the shadows of the tree line. Before him lay an open field that stopped at the walls of Jericho, towering high above the ground. Not long ago, he had led his people across the Jordan River. As they set up camp he had slipped away to scout out the city's defenses.

The trees concealed him from the watchmen's eyes. "This is it," he thought as he strained his eyes to see every detail of the city's fortifications. His scouts had been right. Jericho was well-fortified, and no one was coming in or out of the city's gates. The people of the city knew that just outside their walls lay a mighty army.

Joshua had been studying the city since just before sunset. He watched the changing of the guards and heard the heralds cry out the hour. A stick gently rested between the thumb and forefinger of his right hand. A drawing of the city, scratched out of the earth with the stick, lay on the ground before him. Joshua had been a military leader now for many years. Inside his soul he yearned for the fall of Jericho and the possession of the land promised to him and to his people by God. However, outwardly he could not figure out how to penetrate the mighty walls that protected such a great prize. He wished for a great battle plan; something that would win the fight.

As his eyes lingered on his drawing, he caught a glimpse of someone near him. His instincts took over, and before he could realize what lay before him he found himself in an attacking posture. "Are you for us or against us?" he questioned the stranger.

"No, but as Commander of the army of the LORD I have now come," the man answered.

Joshua fell to the ground in a prostrate position and worshiped. Now, with a spirit of humility, Joshua inquired, "What does my Lord say to His servant?"

Joshua humbled himself before the Lord and obeyed his instructions. God then laid out the plan to overcome Jericho. Joshua did not debate the points of God's plan, nor did he try to interject his own. He had been studying the city for hours and knew that he did not have a plan of action. He was receptive to God's plan and followed it to the letter.

Not only was Jericho a well-fortified city, it was also the first city to be conquered in the Promised Land. It was the first step to be taken to accomplish the overall goal. If the children of Israel had bypassed the city for an easier target, they would have left their backside open to the enemy.

Jericho represented a new level of faith for Joshua and for the people he led. Until this point, they had won battles against small bands of raiders, and the occasional army in the field, but never anything the size of Jericho. Growing in God also means growing in faith. Once we have accomplished the impossible, a limitation in our life has been broken. All of a sudden we realize that the obstacle can indeed be overcome, and we can achieve what we set out to do. When we meet and beat an obstacle and obtain a promise, it is vital to set new goals and reach for them. We will never grow in our spiritual lives if we never desire to move forward.

As Joshua stood by Jericho, he knew that the capture of the city was only the beginning. He was not yet looking toward Ai or the other parts of the Promised Land, because he knew that if Jericho did not fall, the promise would be lost. The world teaches us to keep our eyes on the task at hand. However, is that the way God wants us to view the dreams and promises that He has given us?

The word of God states that you will receive according to your faith. If God has given you a promise and you have faith to receive it, then it is yours. This is true regardless of what may lay before your eyes. You may ask, "If I close my eyes and really, really, really believe, then why do I not see it in the natural realm?" One thing that has kept me from receiving the promises that God has given me is my own perspective.

A few weeks ago I took a vacation, but I did so seeking more than just rest and relaxation. I needed guidance and direction from God. Every year I try to get away from everything and spend time with God. The time is spent reflecting on the past and casting a vision for the future.

As I began my vacation I took out a sheet of paper and wrote down what I wanted from this time alone with God. I wanted to hear His voice, learn the direction for the next year, and most of all see from a new perspective. I had been looking at my problems and promises from my own point of view for years. Like Joshua at the walls of Jericho, I stood trying to figure out how to possess the promise given.

I had spent time reading books, listening to teachings, and trying to plan a way to bring down the walls surrounding my promise. I had tried it all and I had finally come to the place where God wanted me to be: a place of surrender. In my mind, I saw the promise God had given me. However, I did not see myself possessing the promise.

For the next several days I spent time alone with God. I prayed, walked, and talked to Him. I poured out my heart to Him and I found myself asking to see through His eyes. When I prayed, I spoke less and listened more. Sometimes I stayed in silence, but even in those moments, I felt God's presence. It was during one of those times that I heard God's voice say, "The promise you long for is not the end of it all, but the beginning."

I was not sure what He meant, but God reaffirmed the message later the same week. "What happens after I possess the promise God has given me?" I asked a friend. She told me, "Keep on conquering." Then, as if a light had come on in my mind, I understood everything. God had already given me the victory, but I did not allow myself to see it. I was looking at the Promised Land as a one-victory war. It is anything but. God opened my heart to see the whole Promised Land through His eyes.

Whatever promise God has given you, let me assure you that obtaining it is not the finish line. God has even more promises to give you. However, you will not be able to possess them until you realize that God has already given you the victory. I know it can be hard to understand that you have victory when you can't see it with your eyes. Trust me; I lived before the walls of Jericho for years.

WHATEVER PROMISE GOD HAS GIVEN YOU, LET ME ASSURE YOU THAT OBTAINING IT IS NOT THE FINISH LINE. GOD HAS EVEN MORE PROMISES TO GIVE YOU.

Once you see the victory through God's eyes, there is no going back. When you have the vision of victory in mind, your spirit will lift and the strain of the battle will disappear. If you are struggling to see the victory, then spend time before God asking to see His perspective. If you truly seek God, He will be found. That is a promise that He has given, and He will not go back on His word.

Joshua visualized the victory at Jericho and then followed the instructions given. We too must see ourselves standing in victory over the walls of our Jericho. Once we do, we will see the victory come to pass in the natural. God is waiting. Are you ready to see the victory from His point of view?

BEYOND THE WALLS OF JERICHO

Joshua 5:13-15

*13 And it came to pass, when Joshua was by Jericho, that he lifted his eyes
and looked, and behold, a Man stood opposite him with His sword drawn
in His hand. And Joshua went to Him and said to Him, "Are You for us or
for our adversaries?" 14 So He said, "No, but as Commander of the army
of the LORD I have now come." And Joshua fell on his face to the earth and
worshiped, and said to Him, "What does my Lord say to His servant?" 15
Then the Commander of the LORD's army said to Joshua, "Take your san-
dal off your foot, for the place where you stand is holy." And Joshua did so.*

Review Questions:

1. Do you believe that God will only give you the promise He has for you after you do everything right?

2. List three long term goals that you have for your life.

3. When you receive the promise that you are waiting for, how will it affect your long term goal?

4. Are you looking at your promise and goals through your eyes or God's?

Chapter 16
REAPING YOUR PROMISE

And let us not grow weary while doing good, for in due season we shall reap if we do not lose heart.
Galatians 6:9

Using a rag from his pocket, John wiped the sweat from his brow. Farming was hard work, but it was the only work that he had ever known, a part of his life as far back as he could remember. The tractor that he drove had once belonged to his father. His great- grandfather had built the house his family now lived in, and the land he worked had belonged to his family since the early 1800's.

John had just finished planting the seeds that would one day become fields of wheat. He took pride in his work. The satisfaction he felt at the finished planting caused a large smile to come over his face. With his eyes lifted high, he prayed that God would watch over the crop and thanked Him for the abundant harvest to come. As he said "Amen," he placed his worn-out hat on his head, jumped off the tractor, and headed to the house.

His wife, Rachel, knew by the setting sun that John would soon be in. She met him at the door with a cup of coffee and a kiss. "Rachel, this will be our best crop ever. I just know it," John said as his wife returned to the stove. Rachel had heard him say this many times, and every year the harvest was better than the year before. "I am sure you're right," she responded as she placed their plates on the table.

The table always seemed a little lonely at dinnertime now that it was just the two of them. Three other chairs sat around the table, empty since their children had moved away. The two boys had headed off to the service and were now overseas. Their one daughter, Abigail, had gotten married the year before and now lived several states away.

Both bowed their heads as they thanked God for His goodness. They prayed for their family and friends, for the harvest, and for each other. John's Christian heritage, like farming, had been in his family for generations.

After dinner, they sat in front of the fireplace. John began writing out a time frame of what needed to be done in the next few months in preparation for the harvest. It was only September, but he knew that the time for harvesting would come quickly. Rachel sat near the fire, sewing stitches of love into the pants that John had torn the day before. The hours passed, and soon it was time for them to retire for the evening.

The next several months went by fairly quickly. John worked hard on the farm, and it showed in his calloused hands. Rachel also worked hard, taking care of things around the house while staying involved in a local community group. They attended a small country church and could be seen sitting on the third row every Sunday.

Winter came and went, and soon spring was in the air. The stocks of wheat were growing tall, and just as John had predicted, it did look like this would be a great harvest. He knew that from every seed planted a harvest would come, but he also knew that it was God alone who caused the wheat to grow. In planting, John had followed the laws of planting and harvesting that God had established long ago.

It was now late May and soon the wheat would be ripe for harvest. As John stood on his front porch reflecting on the goodness of God, Rachel rushed to him. "John, there is a fire down at the Johnson farm." Without saying a word, John ran to his truck. Soon the only thing that could be seen of him was the dust the truck kicked up as it raced down the dirt road.

When he arrived at the Johnson farm, part of the barn was up in flames. Men were making a line and passing buckets of water as they tried to get the fire under control. John saw Mary Johnson crying as her sister tried to comfort her. "Mary, where is Ben?" John asked. All Mary could manage to do was point toward the burning barn.

Ben Johnson had been John's best friend since grade school. They had been in each others' weddings, and their families always celebrated the holidays together. There was no way that John was going to stand by and watch his dear friend die.

John rushed to the water pump nearby and soaked his clothes until he was wet down to his skin. Once he was covered with water from head to toe he rushed into the burning barn. He tried to see through the thick gray smoke as he kept his mouth covered with a wet rag.

After several minutes John located Ben laying face down near the rear of the barn. Using all the strength he could muster, John propped Ben up until he could get his arm around him. Step by step, John managed to drag Ben closer to the barn door. Soon the men who had been throwing water on the fire could see them. Two of the men raced forward, took Ben, and carried him the rest of the way.

John followed behind them, but not close enough. As he was almost clear of the door, one of the large crossbeams fell. John heard the wood cracking and looked up just in time to see it fall. He tried to step out of the way, but his right leg was pinned under the beam.

The men who had helped Ben out heard the crash, and they turned to see John now trapped. They rushed back and began working feverishly to free him. As they pulled John to safety, they could see that his leg had been crushed by the blow of the beam.

Both John and Ben were soon in an ambulance being rushed to the county hospital. A few days later Ben was released with only minor injuries. John, on the other hand, had not been so lucky. The doctor told him that he was able to save his leg, but that it would take a while before he was able to walk again.

The news crushed John's soul just as the beam had injured his leg days before. Rachel was there beside him as the sentence was pronounced, and she took his hand. Both knew what this would mean. The great harvest, only a few days away, would not be collected. The wheat would be burned up in the summer sun and all would be lost.

As this fact settled upon them, they did what they had always done in trying times: they prayed. Bowing their heads, they thanked God for His goodness. Neither John nor Ben had lost their lives in the fire. If nothing else, that was something to be thankful for. As they prayed, they felt a peace fall over them. They still had no idea how they would make it through the next year, but they now had peace about their situation.

The day after the fire, Rachel had returned home long enough to pack up a few things. For the next few weeks she stayed in town with relatives who lived near the hospital. When John was released from the hospital, he joined her there. He was still unable to walk and had several weeks of therapy ahead of him. He had no desire to return home before he could walk again, and staying close to the hospital made it easier for both of them.

Finally, the day came that John was able to walk again, and he and Rachel decided to return to their farm. As they turned down the dirt road that lead to their farm, Rachel pulled the car off the road and stopped. John had been looking out the window, but his mind was a million miles away. When he realized that the car was not moving, he asked Rachel, "Why have you stopped?" She began to cry as she pointed to their wheat fields. The wheat was completely gone. The fields that had been tall with stalks of wheat now stood empty.

They could not believe their eyes. Pulling the car back on to the road, Rachel drove quickly home. They were met by a host of friends and family as they pulled into the drive. As John got out of the car, Ben embraced him. Ben then led him to the grain silo that was now overflowing with an abundant harvest.

Each person took joy in sharing with John and Rachel how they had helped in the harvest. It was hard to believe that, like angels from above, each person had played a part in bringing the wheat in. Just as John had predicted, it was the best harvest they had ever received.

"Reaping your promise" When you hear that phrase, what comes to mind? Growing up in America, we have been taught that we can achieve anything we put our minds to. This means that whatever goals or dreams you might have, you can achieve them if you work hard enough.

God's promises are not received in the same manner. Promises that are made by God cannot be fulfilled by trying harder or working longer. While God does use the hands of humans to bring about His promises, He alone is able to cause the seed to grow. He alone knows your perfect purpose, and He alone knows the end as well as the beginning. He alone knows what is best for us in life. He knows the perfect timing for every event in our lives. When it is time to reap your promises, you must understand that you are not the one that caused the harvest to come about.

My pastor, Dr. Happy Caldwell, pointed it out simply this way. The seed is given from God to our hands. We must then plant the seed given. God then brings the harvest forth from the seed we plant. Finally, we are responsible to reap the harvest once it is ripe.

HOW THEN DO WE REAP OUR HARVEST?
WE DO SO THROUGH THE WORDS
WE SPEAK.

Words are very powerful weapons in the spiritual world. God spoke the universe into existence, and to this day it continues to expand. After you plant your seed and call it forth, you must continue to say that it will come to pass. It is God who has given us promises about our future. As I pointed out earlier in the book, we must ensure that the promises we are praying for line up with the word of God. It is vital that you understand this down deep in your soul. It is also important to understand that if you are unwilling to plant the seed He has given you, you will never see a harvest. So how do you go about planting your seed?

If you believe God has called you to the ministry, then begin spending quality time serving those already in the ministry. God may well have called you to be a great leader in the Christian faith. However, He will never give you the dream He has for you until you are willing to serve the dream of another. During your time of service, you will learn many things that you must have in order to see your promise come to pass. There are many illustrations of this in the Bible. Joshua served Moses, David served Saul, and the list goes on and on.

If God has called you to teach others, you cannot do so if you have nothing to teach. You need to be willing to plant a seed in the ground of learning by sitting under the teaching of men and women of God. In the business world, no one expects to step out of college into the position of president of a Fortune 500 company. Unfortunately, many people do not understand that this same principle applies to all parts of life.

If you are still waiting for a Godly spouse, then read books, take classes, listen to tapes, and spend time building strong Godly relationships with those around you. The lessons you learn will be vital to your relationship with your future spouse. Do you want to be married to someone who already knows how to build strong Godly relationships? Then why would you think your future spouse would be any different?

If God has promised you a particular job, or that you will own your own business, take time to learn about the area He has for you. According to the Bible, it is God who has given us the ability to make wealth. He has given all of us gifts and talents. Each one is a seed that needs to be planted. Finally, ask God to give you wisdom on how and where to plant the seed that He has given you.

Once you have planted the seed, do not give up on it. Just as a wheat harvest takes time in the natural, so does a supernatural harvest. It may take a short time or a long time, however, if you plant a seed it will produce a harvest. When the farmer plants the seeds for wheat he does not come out a few days later and get discouraged when the sprouts have not sprung up. Sometimes it takes up to two weeks to see wheat begin to sprout. Just as it may take a while for wheat to begin to sprout, it may take some time before you see progress in your spiritual harvest. I encourage you to continue to believe for your harvest. It is easy to believe when you can see things happening step by step. Yet, if you must see to believe, then you leave no room for faith.

You must also be willing to continue to speak over your harvest. Continue to have faith that God will bring forth a harvest from your seed. Also, protect your promise from those that would kill it. The farmer protects the wheat as it grows to ensure that it is not killed off by insects. In the same manner you need to protect the promise that God has given you. This may mean only telling a select few, who will help and encourage you through the process.

There are people out there that may mean well, but will try to kill your promise. Do not be discouraged if this turns out to be a person close to you. Jesus Himself faced this when He returned to the town of His youth. He returned as the Son of God, but the people of the town could only see the son of Mary. In Genesis 27, Joseph shared his dreams with his brothers and was sold into slavery for it. I would suggest that you pray and ask God who you can share your promise with. He will show you when and with whom to share your dream, but you must follow His lead.

How will you know when your harvest is ready to be brought in? In order to know your harvest, you must first know the purpose of the harvest. A farmer knows that it takes a particular amount of time for each crop to come to fullness. Winter wheat is usually planted in September and then harvested in late May or June. The farmer knows that the field to his right is wheat; because that is the seed he planted there. Many of us have planted an abundance of seed, yet we do not know if we have ever received a harvest from it. One reason for this is that, when we planted the seed, we failed to designate its purpose. If we designate what our seed is for when we plant it, then we will know when we have received the harvest from that seed.

ONCE YOU HAVE PLANTED THE SEED, DO NOT GIVE UP ON IT.

Let me give you an example. You desire peace in your family and you decide to plant a seed toward that goal. As time goes on, you continue to plant seeds of love and kindness toward those in your family. When you look back and realize that you have peace, will you not recognize that it is the harvest of the seed you planted? This same principle works in all areas of your life.

I must warn you that the law of the harvest is a universal law that God has put in place. This means that we must be very careful as to what seed we are planting. If you choose to plant seeds of gossip, anger, strife, or any other negative seed, you will receive a negative harvest.

As we conclude this chapter I would like you to remember the words of Pastor Happy Caldwell.

1. God gives the seed to be planted.
2. Man must plant the seed.
3. God brings the seed to fullness.
4. Man must reap the harvest.

Remember to ask God for seed to sow. When He gives you the seed and you plant it, remember to tell Him why you are planting it. As time goes on, continue to thank Him for the harvest that is to come. Continue to speak out in faith when doubt comes about your harvest. Work on areas of your life to get them ready for the harvest. Finally, give thanks to God when your storehouse is filled with the harvest.

I know some of you have been waiting a long time for your harvest. You have confessed your harvest and are tired of waiting. I hope that in the pages of this book you have found ways that you can actively wait on the promise that God has given you. God does not lie. This means that if He has given you a promise, He will bring it to pass. I would encourage you to continue the good fight. Continue to run the good race, and you will reap the promise that you have been given.

Enjoy the journey, learn from the waiting, and prepare your life for the wonderful harvest God has for you. In a day, God turned Joseph from a prisoner to a governor, Moses from a slave to the son of Pharaoh's daughter, David from a servant to a king, and Israel from a people of nomads to a nation. In less than twenty-four hours, you could go from waiting to watching your promise come true.

REAPING YOUR PROMISE

Mark 4:26-29

26 And He said, "The kingdom of God is as if a man should scatter seed on the ground, 27 "and should sleep by night and rise by day, and the seed should sprout and grow, he himself does not know how. 28 "For the earth yields crops by itself: first the blade, then the head, after that the full grain in the head. 29 "But when the grain ripens, immediately he puts in the sickle, because the harvest has come."

Galatians 6:7-9

7 Do not be deceived, God is not mocked; for whatever a man sows, that he will also reap. 8 For he who sows to his flesh will of the flesh reap corruption, but he who sows to the Spirit will of the Spirit reap everlasting life. 9 And let us not grow weary while doing good, for in due season we shall reap if we do not lose heart.

Review Questions:

1. Think about those that are around you. Are they promise killers or encouragers?

____

____

____

____

2. What steps can you take to surround yourself with those that will encourage you along the way?

____

____

____

____

3. Are you taking this trip alone, or have you placed Godly people around you?

____

____

____

____

4. Are you willing to help others along their journey to the fulfillment of their promise?

Chapter 17

A WORD TO THE WISE

"The fear of the Lord is the beginning of wisdom,
And the knowledge of the Holy One is understanding.
Proverbs 9:10

Wisdom is one thing you can never have too much of. The good news is that God has promised us that if we lack wisdom; all we need to do is ask. If, as the Bible states, wisdom is gained just by asking, why do we struggle with waiting?

In this chapter I want to leave you with a few tips that will help you in waiting for the promise that God has given you. When you finish the last chapter, turn the final page, and answer the last question, you may still have to wait for your promise. I hope that, instead of just killing time, you will start Actively Waiting. This means taking an active part in the journey to your promise. Let me try to explain it by a story I was told years ago.

GOD HAS PROMISED US THAT IF WE LACK WISDOM, ALL WE NEED TO DO IS ASK.

There was once an old man who sat on his porch every day. He had lost his eyesight many years before and enjoyed listening to the world as it buzzed around him. The old man was said to be the wisest man in the town, and many times he could be found sharing his wisdom with anyone who would listen.

While he was highly respected by nearly everyone in the town, there were two young boys who only saw an old man. They failed to see the years of life and lessons learned in the man's wrinkled face. Instead, they only saw someone who had lived past his usefulness.

One day the boys found a dead bird and came up with a plan to trick the old man. They wanted to show everyone in town that the man was not as smart as they thought. The boys took the dead bird to him to see if he could tell if it was alive or dead.

When they stood before him, the boy holding the bird in his hand said, "You are supposed to be the wisest man in town. If you are so wise, than tell me if the bird that I am holding is alive or dead." The old man listened for a few moments and answered, "The bird is dead."

His answer was correct and this fueled the anger of the boys. With the dead bird in hand, they stormed off the porch. They had intended to out-wit him, yet they left embarrassed. Like most young boys who lacked wisdom, they did not learn humility from this event. Instead they became even more determined to prove that they were smarter than the old man.

It took the boys a week to come up with another plan, but this time they knew it would work. The plan was to catch a live bird and then take it to the old man. The boys would keep their hands over the bird to keep it still. If the old man said the bird was dead, they would show him otherwise. If he said the bird was alive they would kill it and show him that it was dead. In either case the boys would trick the old man and show him that they could outwit him.

It took some time, but they finally caught a bird and went to see the old man. The boys covered the bird with their hands and tried to keep it as still as possible. One boy spoke and said, "Old man, can you tell me if the bird that my friend holds is alive or dead?"

The old man sat silent and heard the bird fighting against the boy's hands. He knew the bird was alive, but he did not immediately answer. He knew that if he told the boys that the bird was alive they could kill it, but if he told them that it was dead they would show him it was alive. Many minutes passed before the old man spoke. Finally, he answered and said, "The bird's life is in your hands. You must choose if it lives or dies."

The promise that you are waiting for is just like the bird. It is in your hands, and you must choose if it will live or die.

When the first generation of the children of Israel in the desert did not trust in God's ways, they killed the promise that He had given them. When their children grew up they inherited the promise, and they too had to choose. Would they follow God or follow after the way of their parents? Doing what their parents could not, they chose to trust in God's way.

The moment they crossed over the Jordan River, the entire Promised Land did not fall into their hands. The crossing was only the beginning, and they walked into it with faith. It would take many years before the entire

THE PROMISE THAT YOU ARE WAITING FOR IS JUST LIKE THE BIRD. IT IS IN YOUR HANDS, AND YOU MUST CHOOSE IF IT WILL LIVE OR DIE.

land of Canaan was under their control. As you take your first step into the promise God has for you, remember that it is only the beginning. God has much more for you than the one promise you are waiting for.

There is a difference between receiving your promise and possessing your promise. The good news is that God has told us that we will see every promise He has given us come true. We only need to depend on Him and follow all of His ways.

There are several avenues to receive Godly wisdom. First, go to the word of God. Many times the wisdom you are seeking can be found in Scripture. Next, seek Godly counsel from a mentor or someone that you know has a strong walk with Christ. I would suggest not making any big moves without such counsel.

Finally, you should always go to God in prayer. He has promised that He will answer you. When you pray for wisdom, you are like a child asking his parent for guidance. A loving parent would not turn his or her child away; neither will God turn you away. Instead, He will give you the wisdom needed to finish the journey—all the way to the promise fulfilled.

Deuteronomy 34:9

9 Now Joshua the son of Nun was full of the spirit of wisdom, for Moses had laid his hands on him; so the children of Israel heeded him, and did as the LORD had commanded Moses.

James 1:5

5 If any of you lacks wisdom, let him ask of God, who gives to all liberally and without reproach, and it will be given to him.

ACKNOWLEDGEMENTS

How do I begin to thank everyone who has helped me along the way?

To my Lord and Savior, Jesus Christ. I can never repay the price it cost You to save me two thousand years ago, but all I have is Yours. Thank You for being with me every step of the way in this journey called life. Thank You for salvation, strength, endurance, faith, love, hope, and the endless promises that can be found in Your word. It is only through You that I have found the true treasures of life.

Mom and Dad, you raised me to believe in God and hard work. The "never give up attitude" that I saw in you as a child has helped me push on when times were rough. I will always love you.

Emmanuelle and Shirley Cannistraci, thank you for opening your hearts and home to me. How can I ever repay the investment you have made into my life? Thank you for everything

Patch, thank you for all of your hard work on the layout of this book, and thank you for being a great brother in Christ.

Rachel, thank you for ensuring that what I meant to say actually ended up on the pages.

About the Author

Lyle has been actively involved in small groups, pastoral care, singles, and men's ministry for the past eleven years. He has experienced every step of the journey between the promises given and the promised fulfilled. In this book he shares the lessons he learned along the way.

Lyle currently resides in Austin, Texas with his wife, Elexis and two sons.

For more information or to contact Lyle Grimes please send an email to

Joshua2415lg@yahoo.com

www.ingramcontent.com/pod-product-compliance
Ingram Content Group UK Ltd.
Pitfield, Milton Keynes, MK11 3LW, UK
UKHW041939190726
13854UKWH00004B/1687

9 780615 237954